THE
HYPHENATED
AMERICAN

Recent Titles in
Contributions in Psychology

The Five Stages of Culture Shock: Critical Incidents Around the
World
Paul Pedersen

Modern Perspectives on B. F. Skinner and Contemporary
Behaviorism
James T. Todd and Edward K. Morris, editors

Chaos Theory in Psychology
Frederick David Abraham and Albert R. Gilgen, editors

Classifying Reactions to Wrongdoing
R. Murray Thomas

Prevent, Repent, Reform, Revenge: A Study in Adolescent Moral
Development
Ann C. Diver-Stamnes and R. Murray Thomas

Post-Soviet Perspectives on Russian Psychology
*Vera Koltsova, Yuri Oleinik, Albert R. Gilgen, and Carol K. Gilgen,
editors*

Multicultural Counseling in a Divided and Traumatized Society
Joyce Hickson and Susan Kriegler

Cognitive Psychology in the Middle Ages
Simon Kemp

Adolescence: Biological and Psychosocial Perspectives
Benjamin B. Wolman

Soviet and American Psychology During World War II
*Albert R. Gilgen, Carol K. Gilgen, Vera A. Koltsova, and
Yuri N. Oleinik*

Counseling the Inupiat Eskimo
Catherine Swan Reimer

Culturally Competent Family Therapy: A General Model
Shlomo Ariel

THE HYPHENATED AMERICAN

THE HIDDEN INJURIES OF CULTURE

JOHN C. PAPAJOHN
HARVARD MEDICAL SCHOOL

Contributions in Psychology, Number 38
Paul Pedersen, Series Adviser

GREENWOOD PRESS
Westport, Connecticut • London

Library of Congress Cataloging-in-Publication Data

Papajohn, John.
    The hyphenated American : the hidden injuries of culture / John C.
Papajohn.
       p.   cm.—(Contributions in psychology, ISSN 0736–2714 ; no.
38)
    Includes bibliographical references (p.) and index.
    ISBN 0–313–30930–2 (alk. paper)
    1. European Americans—Cultural assimilation—Case studies.
2. European Americans—Psychology—Case studies. 3. United States—
Ethnic relations—Case studies. 4. Irish Americans—Case studies.
5. Italian Americans—Case studies. 6. Jews—United States—Case
studies. 7. Greek Americans—Case studies. I. Title. II. Series.
E184.E95P37   1999
305.8'00973—dc21   99–14837

British Library Cataloguing in Publication Data is available.

Library of Congress Catalog Card Number: 99–14837
ISBN: 0–313–30930–2
ISSN: 0736–2714

First published in 1999

Greenwood Press, 88 Post Road West, Westport, CT 06881
An imprint of Greenwood Publishing Group, Inc.
www.greenwood.com

Printed in the United States of America

The paper used in this book complies with the
Permanent Paper Standard issued by the National
Information Standards Organization (Z39.48–1984).

10 9 8 7 6 5 4 3 2 1

Copyright Acknowledgments

The author and publisher gratefully acknowledge permission for the use of the
following material:

Chapter 5 is adapted from John Papajohn, A case of severe anxiety, in *Intensive
behavior therapy*. Copyright © 1982 by Allyn & Bacon. Adapted by permission.

Portions of Chapters 8 and 9 are adapted from John Papajohn, Ethnic families
and culture change, in *Transactions in families* by John Papajohn and John P.
Spiegel (San Francisco: Jossey-Bass, 1975). Used by permission of Jason Aron-
son Inc. Publishers.

For my grandmother Garoufalia
a reluctant immigrant
whose love made this work possible.

CONTENTS

FOREWORD

John Papajohn has been one of the pioneers in the field of psychiatry who have caused the field to take culture seriously. He has consistently valued the importance of each client's cultural context in his practice and in his teaching. The following chapters demonstrate that expertise in the analysis of cases about third-generation Americans and the ways their immigrant background caused them to alter and adapt to U.S. culture. Each case example presents a puzzle first of all to the subject and second to those of us seeking to learn from that subject's experience. This book builds on the research foundation of John P. Spiegel and Florence Kluckhohn at Harvard University in the late 1950s from the perspective of cultural anthropology.

The book takes a conversational tone with the minimum of references or other interruptions of the dialogue between John Papajohn and you as the reader of this book. In that conversation you will receive the benefit of Professor Papajohn's many years of experience. The title of the book identifies the "hidden injuries of culture" among "hyphenated Americans." New arrivals frequently experience the disadvantages of being new without any of the benefits. Being "different" consistently works against them in their new home. This was especially true for the children in the immigrant families, and they receive special attention by Professor Papajohn.

We know that the children of new immigrants are likely to reject the cultures of their parents and to become instead members of their new home culture. We also know that the children of the immigrant children frequently go back to their roots and the cultural background of their grandparents in order to find out who they are and where they came from. This book is a model in Multicultural Identity Awareness as each different generation experiences the immigration event differently. When you have completed reading this book you will—hopefully—have more questions than you have now before you begin. The task of this book is not to answer your questions but to provoke new questions in your mind about cultural identity, where it comes from and what it means. The task of this book is to increase your awareness of both your own cultural identity and the cultural identity of others. This book provides a conversational model that will lead you to that new awareness.

The team of Spiegel, Kluckhohn, and Papajohn represents a significant position in the combined fields of anthropology and psychiatry. The careful clinical analysis of each case from both the anthropological and the psychiatric perspective combines the roles of participant and observer in a unique approach. The simplistic stereotypes that are often applied to "hyphenated Americans" are rejected in a systematic analysis of each case, leaving the reader to struggle with the complexity of an ambiguous reality. Whether readers approach this book from the perspective of anthropology or psychiatry, they will find the cases valuable teaching opportunities.

As Papajohn points out, "Our cultural traditions, beyond our awareness, have an impact on how we view ourselves and how we experience those with whom we interact." It is essential for each practicing mental health professional to build a platform on which they can stand and view themselves as well as the communities they serve. As you read this book imagine yourself building such a platform for yourself to increase your own multicultural awareness.

Paul Pedersen
Series Adviser
University of Alabama at Birmingham
Department of Human Studies

PREFACE

This book is based on the original research on culture change and mental health in American ethnic groups initiated at Harvard University in the late 1950s by John P. Spiegel, a psychiatrist, and Florence Kluckhohn, a cultural anthropologist.[1] They examined the effect of culture change on the mental health of Irish and Italian families living in the Boston area. Families were chosen in which a child had been diagnosed with a neurotic disorder and was being treated at the psychiatric unit of Children's Hospital in Boston. These were families in which the original immigrants, now the grandparents of the identified patients, were born and raised in Italy or Ireland and had emigrated to the United States as adults. Their children, the parents of the disturbed children, were born and raised in the Boston area.

Spiegel and Kluckhohn hypothesized that the emotional disorder in the children of these families was related to the culture conflict experienced by their parents. Although American born, these parents grew up in ethnic families in which their foreign-born parents had a worldview, a set of values, and specific ways of thinking, feeling, and acting that were inconsistent with what they learned in the "American" schools. The resultant confusion as to how to live manifested itself in conflict between the spouses in these families. Often one of the parents was more Americanized than the other, so that basic disagreements surfaced about how to rear the children. The less-Americanized spouse, for example, as was the case in one of the Italian families, wanted his children to spend more time with the extended family, mainly his parents, while his wife wanted their kids to spend more time in sports and other more individual pursuits. This culturally patterned discrepancy as to what was important was projected onto their son, who was, quite unconsciously, scapegoated. He couldn't do anything that would please both parents and subsequently developed psychosomatic symptoms, constipation, and other physical maladies. Spiegel and Kluckhohn's early efforts were "clinical" studies of an exploratory nature designed to examine the relationship between culture change, family dynamics, and individual psychological disorder in a family member. In their next study of Greek-American families, they employed a more objective, scientific methodology. I joined their research team upon completion of my Ph.D. degree in clinical psychology in 1962.

As a team, Spiegel, Kluckhohn, and I developed an elaborate research design to study the effects of culture change on the mental health and illness of a group of Greek-American families living in the Boston area.[2] In this study, we focused on families with a member who was in a psychiatric hospital. The patients were children of the original immigrants and were then in their fifties. We examined the relationship of their illness to conflicts within their families, and these family conflicts in turn were examined in relation to the stress of culture change, of adapting to the American society in which they now found themselves. Often these conflicts were intergenerational; the children socialized in American schools clashed sharply with their parents in basic issues of living. The parents could no longer expect the kind of respect and submission from their children that they had given their parents when they were growing up in Greece. Their children's effort to "individuate," to become independent "Americans," was viewed as a betrayal, an irrational demand that derived from their selfishness and ingratitude. Dating for women was absolutely forbidden, and no one could expect any privacy, since boundaries between family members were permeable—everyone was privy to everyone else's thoughts and feelings. Some rebelled and separated themselves from their immigrant parents, while others broke apart emotionally from the stress.

We compared this group of families that had a disturbed member with a second group in which there was no history of mental illness. In these "well" Greek-American families, we found that the parents themselves had shifted toward adopting American values. Furthermore, they were more flexible, and their traditional Greek values served as a bridge to American values of achievement. They could, therefore, allow their children more space for individual growth and achievement. The children in these families were more likely to go to college and to be socially upwardly mobile. The parents were able to be supportive and understanding of their children's needs in facing coping tasks different from those they had faced in the rural Greece from which they had immigrated.

This research is described in detail in our book, *Transactions in Families* (1975), a modern approach to studying intergenerational and cross-cultural conflict. In 1979, we developed a training project at the Department of Psychiatry at the Cambridge City Hospital and the Department of Psychiatry at the Massachusetts General Hospital, which was administered through Brandeis University where Spiegel and I held appointments.

The focus now was to apply our knowledge of culture change and mental health in the treatment of emotionally disturbed individuals from different ethnic backgrounds. We were awarded a National Institute of Mental Health Training grant to do this. Our goal was to add a "cultural" segment to the traditional training programs provided at these Harvard Medical School Teaching Centers for psychiatrists, clinical psychologists, and social workers. We did this through the customary teaching modalities such as seminars, teaching conferences, and individual supervision. These efforts, however, were only moderately successful. Although we were welcomed into these institutions and validated by the "power structure," we found that our influence on the content of the training programs in these disciplines was short-lived.

We began gradually to understand the source of the resistance we encountered. There is a reluctance on the part of mental health professionals to acknowledge and accept their own ethnicity as a vital force in their lives. Many were the grandchildren of immigrants who had "made it" in mainstream American society and had spent a lifetime "repressing" their distinct ethnic identity. The reasons, of course, were not hard to understand. Their immigrant grandparents had often been discriminated against for their ethnicity, and their parents had also experienced discrimination, albeit to a lesser degree. These professionals had put behind them the pain of their own American acculturation and had no desire to look back. Furthermore, it was dysfunctional to do so: What could be gained by accentuating cultural differences? What was functional was to focus on sameness, on the shared American values that bound them to their colleagues. The specter of stereotyping ethnic people also held the danger of misdiagnosing them at best or being accused of discrimination at worst. Also, ethnic people themselves didn't want to be identified as such. Some perceived inquiries into their cultural and religious backgrounds as efforts to label them in a negative way. It was no wonder that we didn't get very far with our training effort.

In my own private psychotherapy practice, however, I found the insights and "broadsights" I had acquired into culture as a factor in understanding people's conflicts extremely important and very functional. That is what this book is about. Not intended exclusively for the therapist, this book is offered to the general public in the hope that it will enlighten their understanding of why their intimate relationships sometimes don't work, while at other times and with "others" they do. Our cultural traditions, beyond our awareness, have an impact on how we view ourselves and how we experience those with whom we interact. They constitute a dynamic force that can break through our repression and manifest itself in unexpected and seemingly irrational ways in our relationships. This dynamic force has given me the motivation and the energy to write this book. I hope it will show how cultural factors that generate misunderstandings and conflict can also nurture creative efforts.

NOTES

1. J. P. Spiegel & F. R. Kluckhohn, *Integration and conflict in family behavior report 27* (Topeka, KS: Group for the Advancement of Psychiatry, 1954).

2. J. Papajohn & J. P. Spiegel, *Transactions in families: A modern approach for resolving cultural and generational conflicts* (San Francisco: Jossey-Bass, 1975).

INTRODUCTION

The United States is a heterogeneous society composed of more than a hundred distinct ethnic groups. We have always been a nation of immigrants but our culture in one sense is quite homogeneous. Since the Pilgrims, this country has been populated predominantly by people from Northern Europe—Anglo-Saxon, Protestant, and white. Besides our language, our legal, educational, and commercial institutions have a decidedly English cast. Those who arrived later from culturally diverse parts of Europe—the Italians, the Portuguese, the Germans—confronted a society that initially did not accept them. It was expected that ultimately these culturally different groups would merge, or better "melt," into a common mainstream White Anglo-Saxon Protestant (WASP) society. However, a hundred years after the great wave of immigration at the turn of this century (between 1900 and 1910, 8.2 million individuals immigrated to the United States, primarily from Southern Europe), this has not happened.[1] Despite significant intermarriage among different subcultural groups and of different ethnicities with mainstream "WASPs," Americans remain hyphenated; Greek-Americans, Irish-Americans, and so forth.

This reality constitutes a paradox: an Anglo-dominant society comprised of culturally divergent ethnic groups who have preserved to a greater or lesser degree their "old-world" traditional identities.

This issue has come into sharper relief in the more recent past. In the decade 1980–1990, more than eight million immigrants, predominantly Asians and Hispanics, have immigrated to the United States. This new wave of immigration was made possible by the 1965 Immigration Act, which increased the quotas allowed from these parts of the world. Cultural diversity has again become a vital issue, drawing the attention of the business and educational communities. The demographics of this country have been markedly altered by this new wave of immigration. In the Los Angeles area, for example, ethnics—that is, Asians, Hispanics, and blacks—outnumber the white, Caucasian population.[2] This sociological "paradox" has its psychological counterpart. Psychologists and anthropologists have labeled it acculturation stress. In order to survive economically and socially, immigrants must adapt to the sociocultural reality they find here. This means learning new ways of thinking, feeling, and acting, thereby giving up the old ways they brought with them. This is a complex process at best, since giving up the old ways can mean denying one's cultural heritage and thereby one's identity. This in turn can lead to anomie and despair.

There are those who tenaciously hold on to their traditional customs and remain ensconced in ethnic ghettos, having only minimal contact with nonethnics or mainstream society. Others, however, are highly motivated to succeed economically and socially in "American" mainstream terms and embrace the American Dream for success. They work hard, are upwardly mobile socially, and send their children to college so that they can enjoy a better life than they had been able to as immigrants in their adopted country. The children and grandchildren of these immigrants integrate into American society, where they de-emphasize their ethnic heritages, anglicize their foreign names, and rarely marry partners from their own cultural, that is, ethnic, background.[3] They consider themselves Americans— and of course they are—and often deny or are unaware that their particular ethnic heritage continues to have an impact on their thinking, their feelings, and their behavior. The values that their ethnic parents and grandparents brought to this country continue to pattern their perceptions of how life ought to be lived, and how interpersonal relationships are negotiated as well as their views of human nature and physical nature and their cognizance of time.[4]

This influence becomes especially apparent in interpersonal relationships. Conflicts with peers in school, in the workplace, and in intimate relationships can often be traced to cultural values that are at variance with those of their mainstream American counterparts. Being unaware of this, these descendants of immigrants attempt to understand these conflicts in terms of "personality" differences. Thus these conflicts cannot be successfully resolved because the underlying differences in cultural values are not addressed.[5]

It is in the course of intensive psychotherapy that these underlying cultural conflicts can emerge. This has been my experience over many years in treating individuals of diverse cultural backgrounds. Failed therapeutic outcomes often are the result of the therapist's insensitivity to cultural factors. Therapists who do not have the theoretical orientation that makes it possible to ferret out subtle but important cultural factors in their patients' conflicts are destined to fail.

It will become evident in the case histories that follow that my approach, in addition to being culturally oriented, reflects both a behavioral and a psychodynamic perspective. This is consistent with the integration of these two schools of therapy as described in *Intensive Behavior Therapy: The Behavioral Treatment of Complex Emotional Disorders.*[6] Overt symptoms such as obsessive-compulsive disorder, panic disorder, and others are addressed initially behaviorally; that is, techniques based on Pavlov's and Skinner's conditioning theories are employed to relieve symptoms.[7,8] The therapy does not stop there, however; it is followed by a more comprehensive, insight-oriented exploration in order for the patient to comprehend, in a more macroscopic fashion, the forces that have shaped his or her life and contributed to the development of emotional suffering. Cultural determinants have been demonstrated to constitute a significant portion of these forces. This is the component, as noted above, that is often overlooked by psychotherapists who proceed as if every patient they see has internalized WASP values.

The case histories that follow will attempt to illustrate the importance of cultural determinants in the diagnosis and treatment of individuals with emotional disorders. I hope that these insights will be valuable to people besides those in the mental health field.

Chapter 1 describes the theoretical foundation on which the analysis of the case histories that follow is based. It should be noted that culture conflict is not presented here as the cause of emotional disorders but rather as one parameter in a transacting system of events. There are, of course, psychological, biological, and social-class factors that also contribute to the dysfunction of these individuals and couples.

Each of the next four chapters describes the treatment of an Irish-American, Italian-American, Jewish-American, or Greek-American individual. Colleagues and friends have consistently asked me why I have not included Asian, black, or Hispanic cases in my study. The reason is that the initial research at Harvard was focused on Caucasian ethnic groups. Spiegel and Kluckhohn felt that Hispanics and blacks were already being researched extensively and in depth by others. Also, in the early

1960s, Asians had not yet emigrated to the United States in the record numbers that they have since the redefinition of the immigration laws in 1965. Furthermore, members of these particular groups have sought out treatment in the many clinics staffed by ethnic therapists who serve these populations and speak their native languages. This, of course, is not universally the case and depends in large part where an individual is in the Americanization process.

The three marital cases were chosen because of the cultural mix that they represent. As with the individual cases, I have taken great care to alter identifying characteristics that could violate the confidentiality of these people. The essence of the conflicts described, however, maintain an intrinsic authenticity and integrity.

Each of the individual case histories is introduced with a thumbnail sketch of the ethnic culture from which they derive. These are not intended to be in-depth analyses or exhaustive descriptions. My intent is to highlight generally accepted characteristics of these subcultures. Again these are not stereotypical classifications; everyone from each of the groups is not expected to have internalized these values or to conform to these norms. This is an important feature of Kluckhohn's Theory, on which these descriptions are based.[9]

NOTES

1. N. Glazer & D. P. Moynihan, *Beyond the melting pot* (Cambridge: Massachusetts Institute of Technology Press, 1962).

2. The new face of America—How immigrants are shaping the world's first multicultural society, *Time*, special issue (1993, Fall).

3. M. McGoldrick, J. Giordano, & J. Pearce, *Ethnicity and family therapy*, 2nd ed. (New York: The Guildford Press, 1996), p. 20.

4. Ibid., p. 18.

5. Ibid., p. 20.

6. J. Papajohn, *Intensive behavior therapy: The behavioral treatment of complex emotional disorders* (Elmsford, NY: Pergamon Press, 1982).

7. I. P. Pavlov, *Conditioned reflexes and psychiatry* (W. H. Gantt, Trans.) (New York: International Publishers, 1941).

8. B. F. Skinner, *Science and human behavior* (New York: Macmillan, 1953).

9. F. R. Kluckhohn & F. L. Strodtbeck, *Variations in value orientations* (New York: Harper and Row, 1961).

1

SOME BASIC IDEAS

Florence Kluckhohn, in collaboration with her husband Clyde Kluckhohn, developed a theory for comparing cultures that constituted the basis for our extensive studies of American ethnic groups. It provides a clear framework that allows us to understand the basic structure of a cultural group without requiring us, at the same time, to know all the practices and artifacts of that group.[1]

First of all, Kluckhohn postulated that people in all cultures and at all times had to solve basic issues of living; that is, common coping tasks in certain defined areas of existence. These areas she defined as activity, relational, time, man-nature, and human-nature. Cultures are oriented differentially in the choices they make in solving coping tasks or problems in these five basic areas. In the activity area, for example, mainstream Americans are primarily Doing-oriented; that is, they are oriented to or place high value on achievement as a primary goal in the activity dimension of living. American children are socialized to believe that achievement is the highest good, that it is of primary importance and that one is evaluated on the basis of her/his achievement in the workplace. In American society, we are often asked what we have "done" or accomplished in our lives, whether in business, the professions, or the arts.

The Being-orientation is also present in American culture, but it is second in order of importance. Feeling good, expressing oneself in a way that results in subjective pleasures—be it satisfying basic physical needs like food and sex, enjoying nature, or finding intimacy in interpersonal relationships—is important, but achievement comes first. The spontaneous experience of pleasurable emotions is second.

In the *relational* area of living there are three choices available to people in all cultures—Individualism, Collaterality (Interdependence), and Lineality (Authoritarianism). In American culture, Individualism is clearly our first choice. Independence is a highly valued trait, and we socialize our children from a very early age to be individualistic. This is reflected in our child-rearing practices—weaning and toilet training are practiced at an early age, and separation from the family is learned through a broad range of experiences, beginning with kindergarten and going to camp as early as age six or seven. Parents are sensitive to the functional relevance of their children's being able to "make it" on their own. This is what is required in a technologically advanced culture where achievement requires long periods of working alone in a consistent, persistent manner without needing the physical or emotional presence of others. One needs to draw on one's own emotional reserves to see oneself first through long periods of educational preparation and then through the intense competition that is the mainstay of American life.

Collaterality—that is, cooperativeness or interdependence—is a second-order preference in American society. We need to learn to get along with one another if we are to succeed in the marketplace, in social situations, and in the family. This orientation is based on an egalitarian, democratic view of relationships: that is, we owe respect to one another and thus need to reinforce one another if we are to meet our individual goals. We cannot rise in the hierarchy of a company without the ability to collaborate with our coworkers toward a collective objective of succeeding in the marketplace.

Lineality, or Authoritarianism, is the third and least preferred orientation in terms of patterning interpersonal relationship. We allow select members of our society to assume authoritarian roles, again because it makes functional sense. Doctors in the emergency room performing critical lifesaving tasks, for example, are allowed to be arbitrary and preemptory. There is no time to be egalitarian. This is also the case with the police when confronting a dangerous situation. But often this privilege is abused, and we are quick to call individuals to account, despite their official role.

In the *time* dimension, there are three possible orientations in all societies—Future, Present, and Past. It is the particular preference of one of these over the other that distinguishes cultures. In the United States, a Future over Present over Past pattern exists—that is, Americans are primarily Future-oriented, with Present in the second order of preference, and Past in the last position. It is not difficult to see that we are Future-oriented in this country, that our lives are geared to planning for future events. We plan for our children's education at birth; we insure our lives, our cars, our houses; each day is organized around a predetermined time schedule. We plan for special events months and sometimes years ahead. We need to do this if we are to survive economically and socially in the technologically advanced system in which we live.

We reserve a Present orientation for those times we can relax—at the end of the day, when we are having fun or are on vacation. We let down, stop looking at our watches, and try to enjoy the moment. A life anchored in the present is what characterizes Buddhism, and some people have taken up yoga, transcendental meditation, and other practices in an effort to become more psychologically centered.

The Past orientation is the least functional in a society like ours. We get nostalgic about times past as almost an exotic dimension. We commemorate important national events like the Fourth of July, but we do not make the past a significant part of our current lives, as was the case with Confucianism in pre-Communist China or is the case in modern Greece today, where the golden age of classical times is very much a part of the consciousness of the citizens of that country.

In the *man-nature area*, the three possible orientations described by Kluckhohn are Over-nature, Subjugated-to-nature, and Harmony-with-nature. Americans are predominantly Over-nature oriented. This makes sense in a technological society where resources are available to harness the forces of nature and to find solutions to problems across a broad spectrum, including social and psychological ones. We are a scientifically minded people who believe that every problem has a solution that eventually will be found.

This is not so in rural parts of the world, where a Subjugated-to-nature mind-set has been formed over centuries and constitutes part of the worldview of individuals in these areas. How could it be different in these underdeveloped countries, where the forces of nature determine one's very survival? One can do little to affect the weather conditions that determine the success or failure of the year's harvest. Furthermore, an individual's efforts cannot improve his or her social conditions, since upward mobility in these rural societies is not possible: There is nowhere to go, and people are destined to live as their ancestors before them. In this country, in contrast, the only conditions we can submit to without feeling we could have done more to improve ourselves are death and taxes.

The With-nature orientation is what the term denotes—living in harmony with the natural physical, social, and psychological forces of the world. Again, the philosophy that undergirds Buddhism is consistent with this worldview. It is quite dysfunctional in a technologically advanced society, however. Although we are exhorted by the younger and more adventurous among us to look to the East for more fulfilling ways of living in harmony with nature, few of us are able to do this—even though we sense an essential truth to this view. Instead, we look to developing our "spiritual" lives within our own particular religious traditions.

The *human-nature* dimension allows for three possible orientations: Evil but Perfectible, Mixed, or Good. The distinctions in this dimension are a little more difficult to make, as Kluckhohn didn't research this area as well as she did the others. However, in the United States we tend to view personality as a mixture of good and evil. One is born neither good nor bad; rather, the conditions of one's life determine in what direction one will eventually go. There is good in everyone and even the most exemplary citizen is capable of evil deeds: everyone has the potential to end up a criminal or a productive citizen.

The Evil but Perfectible orientation postulates that we are born Evil but can overcome our base human nature. This notion is embodied in both the Christian doctrine of original sin and in Freud's theory of the Id: Primitive sexual and aggressive impulses constitute the wellspring of our behavior, which through healthy ego development can be harnessed into creative and socially worthwhile directions. Immigrants from Roman Catholic countries bring this orientation with them, as do people from Eastern Orthodox parts of the world, such as Russia and Greece.

The Good orientation seems to be limited to theorists beginning with Rousseau and is embodied in the writings of neo-Freudians such as Karen Horney,[2] who taught that human nature is basically good but that people are corrupted by the civilized societies in which they mature and live.

These value orientation preferences are summarized in Table 1. The Value Orientation Profiles that characterize American core culture are presented in Table 2. They include the contrasting patterns for rural Irish, rural Italian, and rural Greek cultures. Irish and Italians represented a major portion of the immigrants who came to this country between 1900 and 1920, a peak period of immigration to the United States. Greeks also came in relatively large numbers, considering their proportion to the total population of Greece at the time.

The Value Orientation Profiles of Italians, Irish, and Greeks reflect the common rural character of their respective cultures (see the *activity, man-nature,* and *time* areas and the basic differences in the patterns compared with those of "urban" America). In order to adapt to mainstream American culture and to make it socially and economically, immigrants had to make a shift or culture change. They had to adopt more functional—that is, "American"—ways of thinking, feeling, and acting, a process that generated stress and is sometimes referred to as "culture shock."

These profiles provide a kind of X-ray of the cognitive-perceptual structure or worldview of these cultures. The idiosyncratic nature of these ethnic groups will be described and the structures fleshed out in the cases I describe in the following chapters. Here let me point out that while the Irish and Greeks produce identical value orientation profiles in the *relational* dimension, with Lineality in the first position, Irish families tend to be matriarchal and Greek families patriarchal. It should also be noted that Italians in the relational area are first-order Collaterality (interdependently) oriented and differ sharply from Greeks, even though they share common value orientation patterns in other areas and are often viewed as basically similar in terms of family relationships. Italians are interdependent in

Table 1

Modalities	Value Orientation Preferences		
Activity	Doing: Emphasis is on activity measurable by standards conceived as external to the acting individual, i.e., achievement. (American core culture)	Being: Emphasis is on activity expressing what is conceived as given in the human personality, i.e., the spontaneous expression of impulses and desires. (Mexican rural society)	
Relational	Individualism: Individual goals are preferred to group goals; relations are based on individual autonomy; reciprocal roles are based on recognition of the independence of interrelating members. (American core culture)	Collaterality: Individual goals are subordinated to group goals; relations are based on goals of the laterally-extended group; reciprocal roles are based on a horizontal, egalitarian dimension. (Italian extended family)	Lineality: Group goals are preferred to individual goals; relations on a vertical dimension are hierarchically ordered; reciprocal roles are based on a dominance-submission mode of interrelation. (British upper classes)
Time	Future: The temporal focus is based on the future; emphasis is on planning for change at points in time extending away from present to future. (American core culture)	Present: The temporal focus is based on the present; the past gets little attention; the future is seen as unpredictable. (Italian and Latin American societies)	Past: The temporal focus is based on the past; tradition is of central importance. (Traditional Chinese society)
Man-nature	Master-over-nature: Man is expected to overcome the natural forces and harness them to his purpose. (American emphasis on technology to solve all problems)	Subjugation-to-nature: Man can do little to counteract the forces of nature to which he is subjugated. (Spanish rural society)	Harmony-with-nature: Man's sense of wholeness is based on his continual communion with nature and with the supernatural. (Japanese and Navaho Indian societies)
Human nature	Evil: Man is born with a propensity to do evil. Little can be done to change this state, so the only hope is for control of evil propensities. (Puerto Rican culture)	Mixed: Man has natural propensities for both good and evil behavior. Neutral: Man is neither good nor bad innately. He is shaped by the environment he is exposed to. (American core culture)	Good: Man is innately disposed to good behavior. Society, the environment, etc., corrupt him. (Neo-Freudians)

Table 2

Modalities	American Middle Class	Irish	Italian	Greek
Activity	Do > Be	Be > Do	Be > Do	Be > Do
Relational	Ind > Coll > Lin	Lin > Coll > Ind	Coll > Lin > Ind	Lin > Ind > Coll
Time	Fut > Pres > Past	Pres > Past > Fut	Pres > Past > Fut	Past > Pres > Fut
Man-nature	Over > With > Sub	Sub > With > Over	Sub > With > Over	Sub > With > Over
Human nature	Mixed > Evil	Evil > Mixed	Evil > Mixed	Evil > Mixed

Abbreviations: Do = Doing; Be = Being; Ind = Individualism; Coll = Collaterality (Interdependence); Lin = Lineality (Authoritarianism); Fut = Future; Pres = Present; Sub = Subjugated.

their intra-family relationships. The father is like a titular head of the family Lineality (Authoritarianism is in the second position), and decisions are shared among family members. In the absence of the father, the mother and children can make decisions and sustain the family equilibrium. In the Greek family, in contrast, the father is the sole decision maker and family members have a dominant-submissive mode of relating. Obedience to the father is mandatory. In rural Greece the absence of the father through injury or death resulted in basic disorganization of the family. The eldest male child was expected to assume a responsible role toward his mother and younger siblings but was often experientially unequipped to do so.

It should be noted, finally, that a critical feature of Kluckhohn's theory was that the profiles she developed are not to be interpreted as stereotypical descriptions of how all members of a culture think, feel, or act. Her major emphasis was on "variations" within cultures as well as between them. Obviously every society has its rebels and its nonconformists, and subgroups within a culture may operate from a value orientation base quite different from the mainstream. Artists, for example, may be more Being, Collateral, Present, and With-nature oriented than their more mainstream counterparts in professions such as medicine and law.

Next, let us explore the application of this theoretical system in the description of the stress experienced by individuals and couples of different ethnic backgrounds as they cope with adaptation to American society.

NOTES

1. F. R. Kluckhohn & F. L. Strodtbeck, *Variations in value orientations* (New York: Harper and Row, 1961).

2. K. Horney, *The neurotic personality of our time* (New York: W. W. Norton, 1937).

2

IRISH-AMERICAN CULTURE

The major emigration to the United States from Ireland in the mid-1900s was a result of the potato famine in that country. Since then, however, there has been a continual flow of Irish immigrants to the United States.[1]

As a British colony, Ireland was subjected to laws that inhibited the economic development of the southern, Catholic portion of the country. Land for agriculture could only be acquired through inheritance, so that men had to await their father's death in order to become landowners. This left a vast number of Irishmen without regular employment, which contributed to the development of a matriarchal society, since women managed the family and provided the cohesiveness that was needed for its survival. Their husbands' power was diminished by their unemployment, which contributed to their decision to emigrate to the United States.

In the United States, Irishmen gravitated toward bureaucratic institutions and, over time, filled the ranks of the police and fire departments, as well as government agencies. In some

Eastern cities, they gradually acquired political power as well: the political power of Irish-Americans in New York City and Boston is legendary.

Irish-American family structure took on a decidedly Authoritarian caste. It often remained matriarchal, with women retaining the power they had acquired in their native country. Often, however, the men assumed patriarchal positions and their wives secondary roles, although often they functioned as the "power behind the throne."[2]

The Catholic Church, where the hierarchy was predominantly Irish, also served to reinforce the authoritarian structure of the family.[3] Paradoxically, however, high levels of achievement were attained by many whose drive for Individualism necessitated pushing beyond their family's value orientation. While often viewed as rebellion, this Individualism was also applauded and reinforced as a strong sense of ethnic identity. The intense conflict between generations reflects this discordance in values.

In the Irish Catholic view, human nature is viewed as Evil but Perfectible: by the grace of God, dispensed through the Church, one can be saved from original sin. But guilt is an ever-present feature, especially for those Irish Catholics who deviate too far from family and church.

AN IRISH-AMERICAN MAN

Michael Patterson today is an executive in a large computer firm in Boston. He is successful in his career, has a good relationship with his wife of twelve years, has two lovely children, and lives in a suburb of the city.

Michael is a tall, dark-complected, athletically built man in his late thirties, with strong, angular facial features. He relates in an open, honest, and forthright manner. In meeting him, one does not distinguish any characteristics, physical or social, that would characterize him as a hyphenated American. His name certainly does not reflect it, and chances are he would not characterize himself as such unless asked directly.

He has arrived at his current station in life after a long and arduous journey of self-discovery, both in psychotherapy and in his own independent efforts to understand himself and to take control of his life.

Michael's journey began some years earlier, when he presented himself in my office as a referral from a friend of his, a psychiatrist who worked on the staff of a local psychiatric hospital with which I was affiliated. This psychiatrist could give me only a minimal amount of information about him on the phone. He was suffering, he said, from a "post-traumatic stress disorder," he was married, and he earned his living as a singer with a local rock group.

Michael related the events that brought him to my office. The previous spring he had been driving home after singing at a friend's wedding reception. He had stopped at a red light at a major intersection when, without any warning, he was hit from the rear by a car traveling at a considerable rate of speed. He remembered the sudden shock and the sensation of his body being propelled forward by the impact. He also remembered saying to himself that this was a stupid way to die. He managed to grip the steering wheel tightly as he left his seat, thereby reducing significantly the force of his head hitting the windshield. This effort saved his life. When he regained consciousness shortly after, he remembered seeing the face of a man peering through the side window. It was the passerby who had stopped and who had called the police and an ambulance. Members of the wedding party who were driving by also stopped and were hovering over him as he was lifted onto a stretcher. There was a surrealistic quality to the scene as he described it—men in tuxedos and women in gowns around a demolished car. Just as the sun was going down he looked up at the sky, which appeared as a red haze as the ambulance doors closed.

Although Michael suffered a back injury, he was not seriously disabled physically by the accident. He seemed also to have managed the emotional shock well, since he did not experience any immediate aftereffects. Over the next few months, however, he gradually began to notice emotional changes that made him contact his psychiatrist friend. These changes consisted of increased anxiety in two specific situations—driving on major highways and performing in front of large audiences. On the highway he became increasingly tense, expecting to be hit from the rear when traveling at high speeds. He feared that his tenseness would cause him to slam on his brakes suddenly and make it impossible for a car behind him to stop in time to avoid hitting him. He began to drive in the far right-hand lane and at speeds of only forty-five to fifty miles an hour. Each trip to and from the dinner club or function hall where he was performing was an ordeal. He would be anxious for several hours before each trip as well as when anticipating the trip home.

Whereas performing in front of an audience had previously been an occasion for him to feel good because he enjoyed both the singing itself and the applause and positive response he got from the audience, now he dreaded each performance and could not wait for it to end. He anticipated that he would not sing well, that the people listening to him would not like him, and that he would be summarily fired. His anxiety at times became so intense that he worried that he would lose control and run off the stage in the middle of a performance. He could barely continue working at the time he sought treatment for his condition.

In relating these events, Michael was visibly tense and anxious. His tall frame was fixed in a rigid, vigilant posture. He was trying to brace himself to be able to endure the painful ordeal he was going through in reliving these events. In providing him with reassurance and support at this point, I found myself assuming an informal, matter-of-fact posture. I felt immediately empathetic and was able to transmit this without feeling inhibited about transgressing emotional boundaries—that is, without being intrusive. "This man is not a WASP," I said to myself.

In the history that I took in the next session, I learned that I was right. Michael was born in South Boston, a working-class, predominantly Irish area of the city, from which his parents had moved to an outlying suburb when he was five. His father was a high-ranking official in the police department. His mother was a housewife. He seemed surprised when I asked him where his maternal and paternal grandparents were born. He was amused at my surprise in learning that both sets of grandparents had emigrated from Ireland in the early 1900s.

The first order of therapeutic business with Michael was to address his anxiety—his post-traumatic stress disorder, as it has come to be labeled. This term derives from the psychiatric treatment of men and women traumatized in the wars and who have recurring anxiety episodes that render them dysfunctional. The traumas they experienced in combat sensitized them to be irrationally afraid of any situation that triggers memories of what they experienced in the war—such as low-flying planes and loud noises. In some individuals the anxiety can be all pervasive and ongoing so that the individual is unable to function at all in society and has to be hospitalized.

I used a "behavioral" approach in Michael's therapy. He had specifically asked his friend, Dr. Jones, not to be referred to a therapist who would take a "psychoanalytic" approach in his therapy. He was not disposed to probing his unconscious and uncovering the presumed underlying causes of his anxiety. He wanted a forthright, direct approach to the treatment of his symptoms.

Michael had read a great deal about different theoretical approaches in therapy and had settled in a very determined way on being treated by a therapist trained in "conditioning" psychology. In this approach, symptoms are understood as acquired reactions that are "learned" and can be disacquired or unlearned through deconditioning; that is, unlearning or relearning techniques based on the research of Ivan Pavlov and B. F. Skinner. Dr. Jones knew that I was trained in both traditional, or psychoanalytic, therapy as well as what has come to be labeled "behavior therapy." While I was supportive of Michael's preferred approach to his treatment (he was reinforcing my own strongly held biases), I was also aware that in choosing "behavior therapy," he was possibly also consciously wanting to avoid examining aspects of his past that would be disturbing to confront. It turned out that this was indeed the case—but I am getting ahead of my story.[4]

In a series of therapeutic sessions, I addressed Michael's symptoms through the application of desensitization techniques. The first involved direct exposure to the traumatic event through the use of imagery. I taught Michael to visualize (with his eyes closed) the scene on the highway where he was almost killed. He was able to put himself back into that situation vividly by first learning to visualize scenes systematically, employing all sensory modalities. In addition to sight, he learned to include physical sensations, temperature, and smells as well as the shapes and colors of the relevant aspects of the scene.[5]

Michael experienced high levels of anxiety when he succeeded in constructing an authentic image of the accident on the highway. I monitored the degree of anxiety he was experiencing on a subjective scale of zero to 100 (100 being blind panic) in each scene presentation. This method of catharsis is referred to in behavior therapy by a variety of labels, including flooding, "implosion," extinction, and exposure.[6] Some therapists consider it a dangerous method, since they worry that a patient could be overwhelmed by the induced anxiety and decompensate psychologically. In individuals who are otherwise intact psychologically and who do not have a history of serious psychopathology, the method can be enormously therapeutic. This was the case with Michael.

Within a two-month period, during which we met twice a week with repeated exposure trials during each session, Michael's symptoms of traumatic anxiety subsided. He had, so to speak, "stabilized." He could now visualize this traumatic scene and feel no anxiety at all. Outside the therapeutic situation he had relaxed markedly and reported feeling good for the first time in several months.

We next focused on his anxiety when he sang in front of an audience and when driving on the highway. We used the visual exposure method for those two situations as well. In the case of driving, we also employed an "in vivo" (in reality) exposure technique.[7] Each day, Michael agreed to drive for progressively longer distances on the highway he was avoiding. He initially "contracted" with me to drive the distance to the first exit ramp (about four miles), and to repeat this exercise until he felt no anxiety. This is the "extinction" aspect of the exposure method. He contracted next to drive to the second exit on the same highway and to repeat this drive until he could do it without any anxiety. In this manner, Michael overcame his driving phobia at about the same time that his fear of performing in front of an audience subsided, which occurred through exposure sessions in my office that used imagery as the modality for recreating the experience "in vitro" (in imagination).

Michael couldn't believe it—it was too good to be true. I cautioned him that relapses were always possible, even predictable, but that he could reinstate his therapeutic gains by reemploying the techniques—in vitro and in vivo—that he had learned.

Six months after I first saw Michael, his presenting symptoms had been addressed successfully and I was beginning to think about his termination from therapy. Michael, however, indicated that he was not ready to terminate—there were other things he now wanted to talk about.

We talked once a week for the next year and a half. Michael was now able to access events in his past that he had previously completely repressed. His "insights" unfolded in rapid succession as he became aware of events in his past that had had a critical impact on the way he viewed himself and his place in the world, the directions he took in his career, and his relationships with his wife, his parents, and his siblings (he had three sisters, two of whom were married and one of whom was single), as well as his feelings about the Catholic Church. His ethnicity, it turned out, emerged as a critical determinant in the pathways he had taken and his arriving at his present position in life. His near-fatal accident had, in a way, provided an emotional passage into a broad awareness of where he had been and where it was he wanted to go in his life.

Michael rapidly returned to discussing his childhood. He was able to experience anew the rage he had felt at the injustice he experienced in the Catholic grammar school his parents had sent him to. He had been repeatedly accused by the nuns of transgressions others were responsible for; his emergent sexual feelings were associated with a sense of being bad; and guilt became a stable emotional state fed constantly by the nuns and priests. Furthermore, his parents always sided with his teachers when he complained about something that had happened in school.

After graduating from high school, Michael attended a university in the Boston area and graduated with honors. In a real sense, however, although he lived in the college dormitories, he never left home. He visited his parents regularly and remained connected to his Irish-American friends who lived in his old neighborhood in South Boston. In fact, he formed a rock group with some of them. When he finished college, he found himself increasingly involved in music as a career. He wrote music and performed regularly at clubs in the Boston area with his rock group. They gradually expanded their business to include performing at weddings. Michael also played the piano and sang solo at piano bars. Michael had a vague inclination to pursue another career that was commensurate with his university training, but this was not strong enough to motivate him to leave the career path he was on. He immensely enjoyed the camaraderie of his musician friends, many of whom he had known most of his life. He enjoyed the excitement and the "glaze" of the musician's life, especially the adulation of the audiences, whose approval he found enormously uplifting and ego enhancing. He also enjoyed the opportunity his work provided for meeting attractive women. He had dated many women and was able to express his sexuality without much inhibition with the aid, of course, of alcohol. He drank a great deal, which reduced his guilt.

Let me step back at this juncture and examine Michael's history up to this stage of his life in the context of Kluckhohn's theory. It will become evident that looking at the events in his life in their cultural context leads to a much broader interpretation of his life patterns than a purely psychological evaluation would provide. Before doing this, however, I must add that, much later in our sessions, Michael was able to discuss with me the fact that he understood that his mother was an alcoholic and that he grew up, as a consequence, in a "dysfunctional family." A traditionally trained therapist would view this as the major source of Michael's emotional difficulties—specifically, that he was not nurtured properly and so was left vulnerable to anxiety reactions, and that his post-traumatic stress disorder was understandable as a symptom of this vulnerability. While this causative connection is no doubt valid in a basic way, it does not provide the perspective that would make it possible for Michael to obtain the "broadsight" that in turn led to a change in his life pattern.

Let's take a look again at the cultural value orientation patterns of Irish-Americans and flesh out some of the specific ways these are lived out in this subculture.

As described in the previous chapter, the first-order Lineality in the *relational* area is manifested in Irish families in the form of a matriarchal family system. This was not the case in Michael's family. His father was the stable one who kept the family together. His mother was, in fact, dependent all her life on her husband, and her alcoholism enhanced this dependency. This reversal of traditional husband-wife roles in Michael's family meant that his mother's lack of control in the family structure placed the burden of emotional support on her husband, who was not by tradition socialized for this function. That is, he expected his wife to provide the stability in the family, while he earned them a good living outside in the occupational sphere. Since he could not rely on his wife to fulfill her traditional matriarchal role, he had to fill in as best he could. Michael and his sisters formed a strong bond with their father and a lifetime devotion to him.

Looking again at the Irish-American value orientation profile in the *relational* area, note that the second-order preference is Collaterality, or Interdependence. This orientation is evident in the propensity of Irish-Americans to function occupationally within bureaucratic organizations. They are disproportionately represented in the police departments and fire departments as well as in large industrial corporations in this country. Michael's father's occupation is consistent with this pattern. In the religious sphere, Irish-Americans are staunch supporters of the Catholic Church and over-represented in the Church hierarchy. Furthermore, in the Irish-Catholic Church, the interpretation of the Gospels tends to be severely moralistic—especially in matters of sex.

The effect of this moralistic, punitive posture is seen in the difficulty the Irish have in the free, direct expression of feelings.

They are described by McGoldrick[8] as relying heavily on repression (or "denial") as a major mental defense mechanism. Thus, by definition, then, the Irish must be constantly alert to the uncontrolled breakthrough of aggressive impulses. The use of alcohol, the "great disinhibitor," facilitates the expression of both repressed aggressive and sexual feelings. The consequent guilt reactions remains an ever present "curse," which can only be alleviated by the Catholic sacrament of confession.

The Irish have always been great storytellers, poets, and musicians. These creative forms provide a way to express their strong (first-order) Being orientation in the *activity* area.

Michael's talent for music was not entirely an inherited individual trait, though its cultural underpinning was not apparent to him.

These art forms, in Irish culture, have evolved into acceptable vehicles for the sublimation of prohibited thoughts and feelings—often with humor as a stable ingredient. The Irish wake, for example, provides a setting in which grief can be managed through sharing an endless string of humorous stories.

In the context of these cultural conditioning experiences, it is not surprising that the Irish, as was the case initially with Michael, are not amenable to insight-oriented psychotherapy. Their vulnerability to repressed anxiety makes the process of uncovering feelings too difficult. Also, the Irish are not oriented to working individually—that is, on a one-to-one basis—with a therapist toward the future goal of resolving problems (Individualism and Future value orientations are in the least preferred positions in the respective modalities, i.e., *relational* and *time*). Instead, the priest in his divinely ordained role (Lineality) will hear their confession. (Michael's enmity toward the Catholic Church at this stage precluded this option for him.) Also, one can share intimate feelings with lifelong friends, which reflects the second order, Collaterality, in the *relational* dimension.

Upward social mobility through education and individual achievement can be a source of strain for the Irish, since it separates them from their peers and can result in the jettisoning of the support of those they have left behind. This factor can also take the form of intergenerational strain when their parents and extended family continue to reside in traditionally Irish areas of the city where traditional customs are maintained.

In Michael's case, the acculturation process had already been begun by his parents, who left South Boston where their Irish immigrant parents had raised them and moved to a nonethnic WASP suburb. While not exactly "mainstream," their Americanization was well underway by the time Michael and his sisters were born.

Michael's father worked in a bureaucratic system where his coworkers were predominantly Irish-American policemen. They maintained close ties with extended family, as well as links to South Boston, where they made frequent visits. Michael's two oldest sisters skipped college, married, and had children. His younger sister, who went to a Catholic college, had bonded very strongly to her father and had difficulty getting married and moving away—at least emotionally—from her family. These were patterns of living that reflected the continuing impact of Irish values on the life of the Patterson family. However, they did not wake up every morning and declare their allegiance to Ireland, and would have been deeply offended if anyone implied that they were anything but 100 percent American.

Michael had made the most focused effort to leave his Irish Catholic heritage behind him and move into mainstream American culture. Again, this was not a conscious goal-directed effort. It was only in therapy that he was able to understand what his decisions at those junctures of his life really meant. He attended a nonsectarian college, dated "WASP" women almost exclusively, and was determined to follow a professional career path.

The cultural pull, however, was too great, and he found himself in a career that was very much consistent with his Irish values. His friends in this work were almost exclusively Irish-Americans. He had abandoned his earlier decision to become a professional, which created an internal conflict and was a continual source of psychological stress that he was only dimly aware of.

Michael was performing at a local club with his rock group when he met Joanne, whom he married a year later. He was drawn to her for her strong character as well as her vitality and intelligence. She had a mainstream WASP background and was highly individualistic and very achievement oriented. She was working her way up the corporate ladder of the large company where she worked as a system analyst.

Since Michael worked exclusively in the evenings, except for weddings on weekends, he slid very easily into a househusband role, especially after their two children were born. Joanne left for work early in the morning, and Michael took care of the kids until she arrived home in the evening—always after five. While this arrangement was logical and seemed to be working well, Michael became gradually more aware of his resentment. At first he had felt that this was an egalitarian, modern, nontraditional lifestyle that he wholly accepted. But now he began to feel diminished, relegated to a feminine role, especially since his wife made considerably more money than he did and continued to progress in her profession.

His Irish Lineality was having an impact on his assessment of the situation; he needed to exert his authority in the family in spite of his strong, consciously held investment in Individualism and egalitarianism—the American value orientations that he was consciously committed to. It was only after his accident and our "uncovering" therapeutic sessions that he was able to become fully aware of this conflict and to do something about it.

Michael's accident and the trauma it caused him opened the floodgates of anxiety that his unresolved conflicts had generated over an extended period of time. His post-traumatic stress disorder, while "caused" by his near-death experience, was fueled by these "unconscious" conflicts that further intensified his fear of total abandonment—that is, death.[9] There was the anxiety of confronting the fact that he wanted to pursue a professional career in a mainstream "yuppie" profession, and thereby give up the security of his music career that also ensured him the support of his Irish-American friends. He also feared that confronting his wife with the fact that he was dissatisfied with their family arrangement could precipitate a breakup of their marriage.

After Michael had been stabilized for his post-traumatic anxiety through the use of behavioral interventions described above, we concentrated on these three conflict areas in the more traditional "talking" mode of therapy. The three areas were not addressed in any particular order; various aspects of the problems were examined in a free, open-ended fashion.

Michael came to see that his anxiety had a broader base than the trauma of his accident. He had expressed his anger toward the Catholic Church but now was also able to see that his mother's inability to nurture him contributed significantly to his feelings of vulnerability, which accentuated his sense of injustice at his treatment by the nuns and priests. In fact, his mother was still an alcoholic, and he could now openly confront this fact and discuss it with his sisters. He did not feel it was appropriate, however, to discuss it with his father, whose sensibilities Michael felt needed to be respected. These were not matters that children could freely discuss with parents who were in an authority (Lineal) position culturally. His father would view a discussion of their mother's alcoholism as a challenge to his authority in the family.

The complexities of Michael's career direction and the covert effect of his ethnicity on this unfolded at times in quite dramatic ways. He expressed amazement when he discovered that his Irishness was a factor in his becoming a musician, as he had always believed it was an innate musical talent that drew him in this direction. Also, the emotional implications of this choice of career gradually became apparent to him. It was safe, secure—he didn't need to worry much about failure—and his friends and comusicians accepted him for who he was (Being) and not what he accomplished. They knew and had accepted him since he was a child, like family. Furthermore, his work allowed him to express his "Being"—the spontaneous expression of what was a part of him, his self, his talent; it was a pleasurable "now" experience. Though the Present *time* orientation is consistent with the Buddhist tradition that has been infiltrating American life, as in transcendental meditation (Michael was a meditator), Michael never related his feelings about his work to being Irish. He decided to seek employment in a more traditional occupation.

This decision led naturally to the next one—to confront his wife about his dissatisfaction with their family arrangement. She was not very happy about this, and I suggested that she come to sessions with him so that we could examine this problem together. Though Joanne felt that her strong drive for achievement and upward social mobility was threatened, she was also very committed to Michael and their family. She could intellectually accept Michael's arguments—in fact, she applauded his decision—but she sensed the power shift in their relationship that this would entail, and she balked. As a matter of fact, their family arrangement had become inadvertently and beyond their awareness a matriarchal structure consistent with Irish culture. This was why Michael was able to adapt to it in the first place, but now the pendulum, so to speak, had swung in an "American" mainstream direction. Michael was preparing to make a cultural shift as much as an occupational one. He was furthering his acculturation process, which had been essentially interrupted by his opting for a musical career in the Irish tradition.

In our joint therapy sessions, Joanne struggled with Michael's decision, but in the end they were able to negotiate this issue. In her characteristic Future-oriented way, she worked out with Michael the logistics of his also being employed on a nine-to-five basis, such as using a day care center for those periods when neither of them would be home. Michael would drive the kids to school in the morning and to the day care center during his lunch break; she would pick them up from the day care center in the afternoon. She did a "cost benefit" analysis, computing the initial loss of Michael's income as a musician and balancing it against anticipated future earnings.

Michael approached his job search with a good deal of anxiety. After several weeks he was hired at a local newspaper, but the job paid little and was not satisfying. His wife suggested he apply to the training program of a large management consultation firm, which he did. After completing this program, Michael advanced rapidly up the corporate ladder to the position of vice-president that he now holds.

After our joint sessions with Joanne had stopped, Michael and I continued our individual sessions for several months. He was able to use the support he got from me to confront the new coping tasks he had taken on in the workplace. He was buoyed by his accomplishments: he had, in fact, made it in the mainstream. He of course also paid the price of stress in meeting his professional goals. At times he missed his friends from South Boston, of whom he saw less and less, especially when the competitiveness of his current workplace wearied and drained him. He laughed at himself because of the hackneyed phrase that often reverberated obsessively in his head: Michael, you can't—and you don't want to—go home again!

NOTES

1. E. M. Corrigan, *The Irish* (New York: Simon & Schuster, 1970).

2. M. McGoldrick, J. Giordano, & J. Pearce, *Ethnicity and family therapy*, 2nd ed. (New York: The Guildford Press, 1996), p. 20.

3. K. Miller & P. Wagner, *Out of Ireland: The story of the Irish immigration to America* (Washington, DC: Elliot & Clark, 1995).

4. J. Papajohn, *Intensive behavior therapy. The behavioral treatment of complex emotional disorders* (Elmsford, NY: Pergamon Press, 1982).

5. J. Wolpe, *Psychotherapy by reciprocal inhibition* (Stanford: Stanford University Press, 1958).

6. T. Stamphl & D. Levis, Essentials of implosive therapy: A learning theory based on psychodynamic behavioral therapy, *Journal of Abnormal Psychology 72* (1967), 496–503.

7. Wolpe, *Psychotherapy by reciprocal inhibition.*

8. McGoldrick et al., *Ethnicity and family therapy.*

9. Papajohn, *Intensive behavior therapy.*

3

ITALIAN-AMERICAN CULTURE

The major emigration from Italy to the United States at the turn of the century was from southern, rural areas such as Sicily. This culture is characterized by a Being rather than a Doing orientation; that is, major value is not placed on individual achievement, since this was not a functional alternative in that part of the world. The majority of individuals were tenant farmers with limited opportunities for education and upward social mobility. Work was a necessary condition of life; what was most valued was the pleasure of families being together at the dinner table and at the many religious festivals that were celebrated throughout the year.[1,2]

What also made sense was a strong interdependence among family members, nuclear and extended, since survival was contingent on working together in the fields, as well as in other social and economic spheres. Individualism and independence weakened family bonds and were discouraged.

A strong Subjugated-to-nature orientation derived from dependence on the vagaries of nature; once the fields were sown, the weather rather than individual initiative determined economic success or failure.

Human nature was viewed as a mixture of good and evil. In the same family one could expect to find both a priest and a criminal. Early childhood experiences were not conceived as having anything to do with how one developed. Personal character was explained instead as either genetic—"He was born that way"—or alternatively as fate—"it's God's will"[3] (see Table 2).

Upward social mobility, then, for the children of Italian emigrants, required dealing with an intrinsic conflict—that is, the interface of family Interdependence with the Individualism required for educational and career advancement in mainstream America.

AN ITALIAN-AMERICAN MAN

Steven Genovese is a twenty-four-year-old Italian-American man who was referred to me for treatment of a severe case of obsessive-compulsive disorder (OCD). He was obsessed with the thought that his intelligence was radically diminished whenever he masturbated. This was an all-encompassing preoccupation that overwhelmed him when he was in the shower after having masturbated. He felt his intelligence was flowing out of him and that he would be reduced to a state of total idiocy. These thoughts were accompanied by a high level of anxiety, which, when I saw him in the initial visit, had reached a level where his thinking was becoming seriously impaired. He was deteriorating psychologically; that is, his dread clouded his reason. He was becoming paranoid and fearful that he would die and be unable to carry on normal everyday activities.

I arranged for him to be hospitalized at a facility staffed by psychiatrists and psychologists who were experienced in the treatment of OCD. He was immediately put on Anafranil, a medication that is especially effective with individuals suffering with this disorder. (This is a "serotonergic" medication, one that affects serotonin levels in the brain and is in a class with Prozac and Zoloft.)

Steven responded to the medicine within two weeks and to the psychological treatment provided by "behaviorally" oriented therapists. He was markedly improved and was referred back to me for further outpatient treatment.

Initially the major focus of his treatment was the symptom itself, with no effort to understand or get insight into its meaning. As in all cases of OCD, obsessions are followed by rituals the patient acquires in order to get relief from the intense anxiety the obsessions generate. In the case of obsessive fears of contamination, for example, the patient will wash his hands in order to rid himself of the painful feelings of being dirty. This is done compulsively, repeatedly, throughout the day.

Steven's compulsions were in part cognitive, and he got relief by learning to consciously recognize that his reasoning was in fact not diminished since he could still think logically. To support this belief, he would repeatedly do mathematical computations in his head—addition, subtraction, and so forth—until his anxiety was diminished and he experienced relief. Showering also complemented his cognitive rituals, serving the obvious function of decontaminating the dirty thoughts that were generated by his masturbation. By cleansing himself, he wiped away the sin of having sexual thoughts.

The behavioral intervention consisted of a method called "response exposure-response prevention," in which the patient is first oriented to the psychological factors that are maintaining his disorder.[4] The compulsive behaviors that are employed to gain relief from the obsessions paradoxically also serve to reinforce and strengthen the obsessions themselves. Since relief is a kind of reward or reinforcer, it inadvertently perpetuates the anxiety generated by the obsessions. It follows, then, that to eliminate the obsessive worries one needs to eliminate the compulsive responses or reinforcers that follow them—that is, response prevention.

Steven understood this, and we developed a therapeutic strategy together. It was clear that his compulsive "relief" responses needed to be eliminated. Steven agreed that masturbation should not be followed by showering nor by the cognitive ritualistic thoughts, such as the mathematical operations. He was instead to endure—that is, to allow himself to experience the obsessive anxiety that followed masturbation without trying to reduce it. This is called "flooding" or "habituation." Any habit that is not reinforced by relief will lose its potential to cause psychic pain. The individual "habituates"—breaks the habit—in Steven's case, the connection between guilt and a kind of penance.

This procedure is obviously quite painful and its implementation is not an easy or straightforward operation. We approached it in a step-by-step manner. I suggested Steven do the "flooding" only every fourth time he masturbated, then every third time, and so forth, until he was able to do it every time. This was accomplished over several weeks. We met once a week, and we made "contracts" as to how many times he would do the flooding in a particular week. I encouraged him to persist despite the taxing nature of the procedure and also taught him the "relaxation response," a method of relaxing very deeply that is done after each flooding session.[5]

In about three months, Steven's OCD was under control. He reported that he could delay his shower indefinitely after masturbating and had completely stopped the compulsive cognitive ritualistic behavior. Our work together, however, had just begun. Now we began to explore what caused Steven's obsessive anxiety in the first place. A simple explanation was that he grew up in a religious tradition (Catholic) that said masturbation was sinful. His issues were much more complex, however, and he was interested in exploring them with me.

Steven was born in a working-class suburb of Boston. His parents were both Italian-American. Their parents, Steven's grandparents, both emigrated from southern Italy in the early 1900s. Both his grandfathers had worked as laborers in construction businesses also owned by Italians. Steven's father had followed his father into the construction business, where he developed his own company, despite having barely finished high school. Steven's father and mother met in the Italian neighborhood where they lived. Their marriage was a traditional one: Mrs. Genovese concentrated her life around raising their four children, of whom Steven was the youngest.

Steven grew up in the same neighborhood as his parents in a three-decker house that his father owned. The upper two apartments were renovated into a single unit to accommodate their large family. Steven's grandparents on his mother's side lived on the first level. His father's parents lived in the next block.

Not only Steven's grandparents were available to him when he was growing up but also aunts and uncles and cousins who all lived in the same general area. He recalled experiencing the warmth and caring and protection of this large extended family.

Steven was a good student and graduated from the local Catholic high school as valedictorian of his class. His teachers, primarily nuns and brothers, encouraged him to apply to colleges to further his education. He applied to and was accepted at a prestigious Ivy League college, which he chose to attend over the protestations of his teachers, who strongly recommended Catholic institutions.

His parents, especially his father, had mixed feelings about his going to college at all. They were proud of his being accepted to such a well-known school, but really preferred that he join the family construction business. Steven, however, was determined, and his parents finally gave their blessing.

The summer before leaving for college, which was located six hours away by car from Boston, Steven began to experience an uneasiness he could not quite understand. He was excited about going away, but as the prospect came closer, he became progressively more anxious. He was confused by this and could not identify a cause. His anxiety intensified as the day approached when he was to leave, and after his father had left him alone on the college campus, Steven's anxiety turned to dread. He felt alone for the first time in his life. He had a strong impulse to take the next train home, but was too embarrassed, and he managed somehow to contain his panic. His roommate was affable, and when classes began Steven immersed himself in his studies, which helped him to settle down more. His highly honed study skills enabled him to distract himself from feeling lonely. He also made friends easily, and this, combined with frequent phone calls home, enabled Steven to finally adjust and in fact enjoy the academic life of the college.

His relationship to women at the college followed a pattern that had developed during his high school years. He socialized with them in groups, enjoying weekend parties but rarely dating women individually. He was excited by them sexually but was too inhibited to approach them in this fashion. His religious upbringing affected him in ways that precluded having sexual intercourse outside of marriage. His friends could hardly believe him. They shared their exploits with him, which caused him extreme pain because of the effort it took to suppress his own sexual impulses. He managed to do well in his studies despite this continual added stress.

By his senior year, however, Steven's defenses began to fail him. It was not only the pressure of his repressed sexuality but also the fact that his college career was coming to an end and he had no clear career direction in which he wanted to go. He had majored in English literature, but all he was sure of was that he didn't want to go into the construction business with his father.

He also now began masturbating, at age twenty, which made him feel very guilty. His efforts to manage this guilt, first by showering and then through cognitive rituals, began to take form. By the time he graduated, his OCD symptoms were in full force.

Steven moved back home to his parents' house and began looking for a job—only vaguely conceived—in the banking industry. He recommended his socializing with friends and relatives from his home neighborhood, which settled him somewhat emotionally but not enough. His distress increased, and each time he masturbated he engaged in the anxiety relief rituals he had learned. But they too were ceasing to have the calming effect they had before. It was at this point that Steven was referred to me by the doctor to whom his mother had taken him for help.

It was surprising to me that Steven had so little insight into the relationship between the life events that he had shared with me and the anxiety that had engulfed him. For Steven, the notion that his separation from family and friends when he went to college caused him to be anxious was a novel concept. His interdependence with his extended family was for him a natural condition of life that he assumed was the same for all people. He had not been socialized for individualism and independence, so that when he found himself, at the age of seventeen, entering an Ivy League college where these were the dominant values, he was at a total loss as to how to cope emotionally. He had not acquired the capacity to draw on his own internal resources for sustenance and support when facing the challenges of college life, especially in the social arena. He felt deeply lonely in the absence of his immediate and extended family. He felt like a stranger in a foreign land populated in large part by WASPs, who seemed distant to him emotionally. They recoiled from his efforts to get close to them because he was unfamiliar with those subtle but important interpersonal cues that would have made this possible. He did not know that "Americans" do not share intimacies easily, and only after they have built up trust in someone, often after a considerable period of time.

Steven was confused; intimacy with his neighborhood friends was a given; it did not evolve over time but was a camaraderie that was intrinsic to being Italian, especially within the extended family. There was no need to prove oneself worthy of trust. Steven was helped in this situation by his highly honed study skills, which enabled him to contain his anxiety by being effective and successful in his academic work. He was at a loss when it came to forging relationships with women, and especially in dealing with his sexual impulses. When he finally allowed himself to masturbate, he was overwhelmed by guilt. His OCD symptoms developed in an effort to control this anxiety and guilt.

Gradually, in weekly psychotherapy sessions, Steven was able to take distance from this and begin to understand what was happening to him. His high level of intelligence facilitated the therapeutic process, and he could understand intellectually the difference between his own ethnic values and those of his contemporaries, who were from mainstream middle-class American culture. This intellectual understanding freed him to undertake, in the course of therapy, the individuation process that had not been possible through the socialization process provided within his family. While Steven's OCD symptoms had subsided through the "flooding" and other behavioral interventions, he still needed to learn more independent modes of living. He was gradually able to feel less anxious when he was alone and made a major step in this direction when he moved out of his parents' house into an apartment of his own. This took a considerable amount of coaxing on my part, which was countered by his family's protests that he should wait until he married to move out.

From his new apartment in Boston, Steven initially made frequent trips back home. Over time these visits became less frequent, as he became more acclimated to living alone. Fortunately he got a job at a bank shortly after moving to Boston, which constituted a major breakthrough in that it made it possible for him to relate to coworkers in social situations and set the stage for dealing with his sexual conflicts.

Steven met attractive women at the bank, and for the first time in his life he began "real" dating. He was quite awkward at first, more like a fourteen-year-old than a twenty-two-year-old. Nevertheless, he was able to develop a warm relationship with one woman, and the prospect of having sexual intercourse loomed as a major emotional hurdle. He was clearly not ready for this, and I suggested that he wait until he felt less anxious about it. He disregarded my counsel and came to the next session looking quite energized and happy. He reported that he was quite surprised by his capacity to perform sexually but, more significantly, by the fact that he had experienced very little guilt.

I believe that his capacity to perform sexually was due to two major factors. The first was the desensitization of his masturbation guilt through the flooding technique employed in treating his OCD symptoms. The second was the individuation process that was accomplished through the insight-oriented psychotherapy that followed. Steven was freed from his terrible abandonment fears that were activated by masturbation (that God would condemn him to eternal Hell) and from his internalized belief that he could not exist without the continual presence of his immediate and extended family; that is, his separation anxiety.

Steven's first sexual experience did not consolidate his relationship with his girlfriend. It soon became clear there was little else that bound them, and the relationship became platonic. He dated other women, gradually growing emotionally and becoming able to appreciate them in other than sexual ways. Whereas Steven had previously conceived of sex as a sinful act that was to be sharply differentiated from loving feelings toward a woman, he was now able to experience genuinely loving feelings and to merge these with sexual impulses.

Steven did not become alienated from his family. At the onset of the individuation process he felt some anger toward his parents because of their overprotection and lack of understanding of what he needed in order to grow up emotionally. This anger was especially directed toward his father, whom Steven felt had not spent enough time with him when he was growing up. This phase quickly passed, however, as his insight into the cultural factors that shaped their relationship and his life deepened. His affection for his parents in fact also deepened, and he still turned to them for emotional support at times, though in a quite different, less dependent fashion. He was now able to turn to them appropriately for love and affection and support in times of stress. They, too, became accustomed to his being away, and expressed their joy at his career successes.

NOTES

1. J. Giordano, *The Italian American catalog* (New York: Doubleday, 1986).

2. L. Barzini, *The Italians* (New York: Atheneum, 1964).

3. J. Papajohn & J. P. Spiegel, Contrasts in Italian and American values, *Transactions in families* (San Francisco: Jossey-Bass, 1975), pp. 97–111.

4. J. Papajohn, A case history of a person with obsessive ruminations, *Intensive behavior therapy* (Elmsford, NY: Pergamon Press, 1982), pp. 67–85.

5. H. Benson, *The relaxation response* (New York: Avon Books, 1975).

4

JEWISH-AMERICAN CULTURE

Jews have come to the United States from all parts of the world. As early as the 1700s, a synagogue founded in Providence, Rhode Island, was visited by George Washington.[1] In the nineteenth century, a large group of mercantile Jews immigrated from Germany and other Western European countries, while the surge of immigration from Eastern Europe at the turn of the twentieth century consisted primarily of Jews from rural areas.[2,3]

In the *activity* area, Jews are clearly Doing oriented, with high motivation for achievement and upward social mobility. In the *relational* area, Collaterality (Interdependence) and Individualism seem to be of equal strength. Jewish children are socialized both to form close bonds between family members and to develop a strong motivation for economic and social success in American society.[4] There is in this an inherent conflict, since "making it" in American cultural terms also requires separation from family and immersion in mainstream values. This conflict is often mitigated, however, when Jewish men and women effectively negotiate their professional and business worlds while maintaining close bonds with both their nuclear and extended families. They support their temples and invest emotionally and financially in efforts to promote Jewish causes. They gain emotional sustenance from the Jewish community while investing themselves totally in American society.

Their *man-nature* orientation is clearly Over-nature, that is, that problems have solutions. Anti-Semitism, for example, is viewed as a problem that must be combated and not yielded to. Their view of *human-nature* is mixed. People develop good or bad characters by virtue of their early family environments. Dysfunctional individuals are viewed as psychologically disabled and in need of help from mental health specialists, which reflects the Over-nature orientation.

A JEWISH-AMERICAN WOMAN

Dianne Kaplan had stopped her car at a light when she was rear-ended by another car. She was jolted by the impact but was held firmly by her seatbelt. It was a minor hit; her car was not damaged, and she did not even bother to exchange information with the other driver.

A week later, however, Dianne began to experience dizziness and an overwhelming fear about leaving her house to go to work. She had not experienced any apparent injury from the accident, but her husband insisted that she have a neurological examination because of the possibility that whiplash was having a delayed effect. Her family doctor referred her to a neurologist, who performed the usual clinical tests, as well as an M.R.I. All the tests were negative. Her symptoms of dizziness and anxiety, however, persisted. Her cousin, a psychologist, suggested she see a behavior therapist for the treatment of her "phobia."

Dianne is a twenty-eight-year-old Jewish-American woman of average height, somewhat underweight, dark complected with deep blue eyes and an angular face. She presents in a tense, restive manner, moving constantly on the couch, at times standing up and sitting down to relieve her tension. Her agitation was also evident in her speech, which was rapid and at times difficult to understand.

She reviewed the events leading to her making the appointment with me. She was not at all sure she had a psychological problem and was considering consulting another neurologist, since she was convinced her symptoms had a physical basis as yet undetected. The accident must have caused some kind of injury to her brain, she thought. Furthermore, her phobic symptoms had abated somewhat over the past week. She had driven herself to my office and was relying less and less on her husband to drive her to work.

I suggested that, while a neurological consult made sense, we could proceed to consider psychological causes as well. She reluctantly agreed. I proceeded to take a history.

Dianne is the oldest of three children; she has a sister who is two years younger, and a brother who was born when she was twelve years old. Her parents are both college educated; her father is a banker and her mother an accountant. Her four grandparents are alive and well and living in the same town as her parents in another state. Her paternal grandfather is a tailor who has his own tailor shop. He emigrated to the United States from Russia with his wife in the early 1920s. His wife works with him in the shop, which frees him to go to the temple daily to read the Talmud and pray. Her grandfather on her mother's side also emigrated from the Ukraine during the same period, when he was twelve. Shortly after arriving in the United States he got a job in the wholesale food industry doing menial work. He later started his own wholesale vegetable business and married the sister of one of his friends.

Dianne's mother does not get along well with her mother-in-law, whom she experiences as controlling and manipulative. Dianne has been exposed to her mother's complaints about her grandmother ever since she can remember, but her father maintains close contact with his aging parents, looking in on them regularly and inviting them often for dinner.

Dianne's mother is very close to her own mother, however. When Dianne was growing up, her maternal grandmother often babysat her and her siblings, and they still maintained a strong bond.

Strong emotional bonds in fact characterize this extended family across three generations. Their interdependence constitutes a salient feature of the social context of their lives. This solidarity is enhanced by their strong commitment to their Jewish heritage, although, except for the paternal grandfather, they attend temple principally only on the High Holidays and for weddings and bar and bas mitzvahs. Their Jewish identities are clearly forged.

This became very clear to Dianne when she began dating in high school, and her father forbade her to go out with Gentile boys. This enraged her and she openly rebelled. The conflict continued through her college years. She dated Jewish and non-Jewish men indiscriminately and let her father know about it. At one point they stopped talking to each other for almost a year. Her father would not give in and persisted in his disapproval. Finally Dianne capitulated, but she harbored a deep resentment toward her father. She agreed not to date non-Jewish men, but did so secretly anyway.

After her graduation from college, Dianne moved to Boston and rented an apartment with a girlfriend who had been a classmate. She got a job as a paralegal in a large law firm and continued to date. She became seriously involved with a non-Jewish man, who in the end rejected her. It took her a while to get over him, and then she met Jonathan, the brother of a coworker. She quickly felt that he was "the one." After a relatively short court-ship they became engaged and were married in less than a year.

Jonathan is Jewish. He is five years older than Dianne and is a mid-level manager in a Boston-based corporation. His parents are also college educated and his father, a chemist by profession, founded his own chemical manufacturing company.

At the time Dianne was rear-ended in her car, they had been married for a little less than a year. The marriage was going well, and they had been discussing Dianne's getting pregnant so they could get their family started.

I asked how she felt about this decision. She became impatient with my probing, and her resistance increased so much that she decided to terminate therapy after only four sessions.

Approximately one year later, Dianne called me to set up another appointment. Her anxiety, she told me on the phone, had gotten worse. She informed me in the next session that she was six months pregnant and that she couldn't understand why she wasn't happy about it. Her somatic concerns had intensified significantly. She thought she might be going blind, since at times her vision was blurred. She had consulted an ophthalmologist, who assured her she had no vision problem. A persistent sore throat convinced her she had cancer, but the specialist she saw could not find any pathology. Her arms had become covered with a rash she was certain was skin cancer. The dermatologist told her it was psychogenic and that she should consult a psychotherapist. That's when she decided to call me again.

Dianne still resisted therapy. She was convinced that her anxiety was reality based, that she was destined to be stricken with some serious illness. But when I asked why she thought this, she drew a blank. Initially my efforts to connect her symptoms to stress produced further denial. She had a happy marriage and wanted to start a family, period.

Dealing with Dianne's denial in the following sessions was a difficult, painful process for both of us. I took a supportive stance and built a strong therapeutic alliance with her. I taught her to relax using Benson's Relaxation Response[5] and also employed the flooding technique,[6] instructing her to set time aside each day to sit quietly and allow herself to experience, in her mind, the full extent of her anxious thoughts. The anxiety generated in this way dissipated over a twenty-minute period of "exposure." In other words she habituated, essentially diminishing the intensity of her anxiety by "facing it down."

These techniques worked to a significant degree; she was markedly more comfortable during the day, and her somatic symptoms decreased in intensity and frequency. Any insight, however, as to the cause of her anxiety continued to elude her. She could not see any connection between her somatic symptoms and the stress of being pregnant. This would come only later, after she had given birth and settled down to attend to her newborn infant.

Dianne terminated this phase of treatment about a week before she delivered and resumed therapy six months later. She reported that her delivery had been difficult and that her husband had been extremely supportive. She was not happy, however, about the fact that she felt he was in many ways detached from their child, a boy. He helped with the night feedings but only reluctantly. In addition, a long-simmering resentment had become a major preoccupation for her. Dianne felt strongly that she needed her mother's help in taking care of the baby and that her grandmother would also be able to help, but Jonathan refused to even consider her desire to relocate to her parents' town.

Jonathan tried to reason with Dianne that he was advancing in the corporation, which did not have a branch in her parents' town. If they moved, he would have to forfeit years of hard work and the prospect of advancement.

Dianne thought this was a selfish position. She viewed him as authoritarian and controlling, characteristics she had not seen in him before. She became increasingly dissatisfied with him, their relationship became strained, sexual relations were infrequent, and her somatic symptoms, which until now had abated, returned in full force. Thus she called me for another appointment.

As Dianne related the events described above, she wondered whether she would be able to stay with a man who was so insensitive to her and to their child. She visited her parents frequently, which was a relief for both Dianne and Jonathan. Her parents were very loving and doted on her and the baby. Her mother, hearing her complaints about her husband, revealed that she had always had misgivings about him. This reinforced Dianne's ambivalence and exacerbated her negative feelings toward Jonathan. He felt this, which caused him in turn to distance himself more. His tolerance for her constant complaining about her bodily symptoms was exhausted; he didn't want to hear about them anymore. He also resented paying for the endless number of medical specialists she had consulted.

Dianne's main symptom now was her sore throat. She eventually found an internist who confirmed that her condition warranted laser treatment to shrink a "tumor" that was causing the problem. Two days before she was to have the procedure, her symptoms disappeared.

I resumed the behavioral interventions described above and Dianne's anxiety came under control. The sudden disappearance of her somatic symptom, the sore throat, caused her to consider that there might in fact be psychological factors related to her medical problems.

While she continued to insist that her husband was the problem, Dianne was also progressively able, over many sessions, to consider a broader range of causative events. She was able to see, finally, that the onset of her distress coincided with her decision to become pregnant. Prior to that time, her relationship with her husband was fine. They were very close, did everything together, socialized little with others, except family, and had frequent and satisfying sexual relations. The automobile accident, she now saw, was a trigger but not the cause of her somatic symptoms. But why? What was going on?

It took many sessions and a lot of work for Dianne to gain a broader understanding of what was happening to her. Her resistance to psychological interpretation was granitic. She was firmly "in denial." She countered each interpretation from me with a counter interpretation that neutralized my own. She did not feel entrapped by the baby; she loved him. Her husband was the problem, as he was not helpful with the baby.

Gradually, however, her defenses began to give way. She discovered that she married someone who was not only Jewish but who was in many ways very much like her father. She experienced him on the one hand as a "mensch" and on the other as very controlling. Her marriage, then, replicated much of what she had experienced growing up—a continual struggle over control with her father. She realized that she often gave in to Jonathan when differences arose and would then feel defeated and angry.

Their marriage also replicated many of the patterns she had experienced growing up in her extended family. Their social life was, as noted above, limited to each other and to family visits to both their sets of parents. They did not relate to any other social network. Both had friends at work but never considered socializing with them.

We traced the source of Dianne's anxiety to a catastrophic sense of being engulfed in her marriage. She realized that by marrying she had forfeited a deep desire to go to law school. They could not afford to do without her salary; Jonathan had made this clear. The decision to start a family compounded and intensified her fear of entrapment. They could no longer do the recreational things together that had afforded her some relief from her sense of entrapment, but her denial did not allow her to see this. Her strong drive for individuation, that is, her desire to go to law school, was submerged by the conflicting ideal of being a good wife and mother—the ideal set by her Jewish mother and grandmother. When her children were born, Dianne's mother had given up her job as an accountant and devoted herself full time to her family.

Dianne, then, was torn between two patterns of living that were determined by Jewish and American cultural values. While achievement is highly valued in Jewish culture, so is interdependence among family members. Since achievement is based on independence and individualism, the conditions for intrapsychic conflict are set, especially for Jewish women. A price has to be paid for this conflict; in Dianne this took the form of anxiety expressed through somatic symptoms. Her family, that is the family she grew up in, identified strongly with Jewish culture even though they functioned in American middle-class society.[7] Her father was able to realize his aspirations in the wider American arena and yet return home at night to a warm, cohesive Jewish family environment, since his wife had abandoned her own career goals. Jonathan's situation was not as simple. Dianne's aspirations were submerged, and they surfaced in the form of intense anxiety when she began to experience the fact that she was becoming progressively more contained by motherhood and wifehood, from which there was no ready escape.

It was only when her denial began to give way that Dianne was able to see this. She was also able to see that her drive for independence and individuation had begun earlier, when in her adolescence she dated Gentile—that is, "American"—men. It was typical adolescent rebellion but with a definite cultural caste.

She felt liberated by these "cultural" insights and her symptoms again abated. She began to see Jonathan in a different light, and his flaws seemed less important. She again broached the subject of her desire to go to law school, and having experienced her renewed warmth and caring, he was able to discuss this with her. While they agreed her desire would have to be postponed for the immediate future, he did foresee how they could plan for her to go part time. Dianne relaxed even more, their sex life picked up again, and they began to broaden their social network, inviting friends to dinner and making other social engagements with them.

Dianne was also able to understand her mother's desire to keep her close and then began to take some distance from her. Her visits home became less frequent, and she was able to set limits on her mother's criticism of Jonathan. For the first time, she was able to make it clear she was strongly allied with him. Her mother adjusted, as she did not want to jeopardize her relationship to her new grandson.

NOTES

1. E. Faber, *A time for planting: The first migration, 1645–1820* (Baltimore, MD: Johns Hopkins University Press, 1992).

2. H. R. Diner, *A time for gathering: The second migration, 1820–1880* (Baltimore, MD: Johns Hopkins University Press, 1992).

3. S. Goldstein, *Profile of American Jewry: Insights from the 1990 national Jewish population survey* (New York: Center for Jewish Studies, City University of New York, 1993).

4. F. Herz & E. Rosen, Jewish families, in M. McGoldrick, J. K. Pearce, & J. Giordano (Eds.), *Ethnicity and family therapy*, 1st ed. (New York: Guildford Press, 1982), pp. 365–392.

5. H. Benson, *The relaxation response* (New York: Avon Books, 1975).

6. T. Stamphl & D. Levis, Essentials of implosive therapy: A learning theory based on psychodynamic behavioral therapy, *Journal of Abnormal Psychology 72* (1967), 496–503.

7. S. D. Pergola, Pattern of American Jewish identity, *Demography 17* (1980), 261–273.

5

GREEK-AMERICAN CULTURE

At the turn of the century, Greek immigrants to the United States, who were predominantly from rural areas of Greece, brought with them a strong sense of ethnic identity. They perceived themselves as inheritors of the illustrious culture of ancient Greece, which included placing a high value on individual achievement. This orientation dovetailed perfectly with American individualism and entrepreneurship. Paradoxically, their family structure was decidedly patriarchal; the father maintained unchallenged power over his wife and children—not fertile ground on which to prepare for a life of individual achievement.[1,2,3]

This intrinsic conflict in values, however, did not diminish the drive to succeed economically, though it did exact an emotional price. The immigrant men rapidly started their own businesses, primarily in the food business. Their children had to negotiate their internal drive to succeed with being socialized in the family to be respectful and to obey authority. They managed to go to good colleges and to become integrated into the broader "American" social system. Family bonds remained strong, but again, independence was a necessary condition for individual achievement, and so separation was accomplished at an emotional price; that is, in anxiety that manifested itself in a variety of symptoms.[4]

A GREEK-AMERICAN MAN

Bill Anastos was early for his first session with me. He is a tall, dark-complected man with brown eyes, who appeared to be somewhat underweight. He wore dark-rimmed glasses. What impressed me most was the almost childlike, wide-eyed passivity that characterized his manner of relating to me; he hung on my every word. Bill, who was twenty-four years old, told me right off that he had postponed a move to the West Coast for a month, where he planned to visit his brother and sister. His brother was seven years older, and his sister was five years older. This gave us a total of eight sessions to focus on the problem he wanted help with—his anxiety in job interviews.

As I began the process of identifying the precipitating factors for the onset of his panic and clarifying his reactions in the job interview situations, I took a brief history. I also began to orient him into a behavioral way of conceptualizing his difficulties, including some techniques for managing his anxiety. I asked Bill to describe his most recent experience of being anxious in an interview. About six months earlier, he had applied for a job with a major Boston department store chain. He was a college graduate with a major in liberal arts and wanted to be trained for a management position. He had submitted a written application for the store's management training program; it was during a phone call from the company's secretary to set up an interview with the personnel director that Bill's anxiety began to surface. During the following week his anxiety mounted, as he thought of the interview date getting closer and closer, day by day, hour by hour. The mere image of himself in the interview situation would trigger the anxiety, which included thoughts of being evaluated and failing. The night before the interview he slept very little, although he drank scotch after supper in an effort to calm himself. He awoke the next morning with a deep sense of impending doom, a feeling that persisted on the way to the interview. He almost rammed into a car that stopped ahead of him for a red light. While waiting in a reception area, Bill was barely able to contain the trembling in his legs and arms, and the thought that other people in the reception area might notice intensified his panic. After he had waited for ten minutes, his anxiety had become so overwhelming that he felt sure he was going to die. He got up and bolted from the building.

Since that incident, Bill had been unable to even think of applying for another job; the words "help wanted" in the newspaper were enough to trigger his anxiety. He was understandably worried about what would happen when he got to California. I told him I would help him learn ways to manage his anxiety by substituting alternative relaxation reactions to the same situations. Bill could only vaguely understand this, but he was somewhat reassured by knowing that his was a condition I had treated before and that I felt I could help him.

Bill was employed by his uncle, who owned a large, successful restaurant south of Boston. He had worked there summers during his college years and for the two years since graduation. He had started out as a busboy, worked up to a waiter, and for the last year had been maitre d'. He made good money, and his uncle, who was getting old, had implied that should Bill agree to remain permanently, he would make him a partner in the business. Bill was tempted; he felt comfortable in his work environment, where most of the waiters and chefs were Greek or Greek-American, and he was treated with respect. He was accepted because he was one of them and was supported for being who he was, rather than solely for what he achieved in his work. This was consistent with the Greek norms of culture that patterned relationships in his family. His job situation was essentially an extension of his Greek family. It provided an accepting, supportive environment and shielded him from the stresses incumbent in "making it" occupationally and socially in the broader American social system.

Bill, however, had been socialized in two cultures. He had also learned to value achievement in middle-class American terms. As a college graduate, he could not remain content with his job at his uncle's restaurant. He felt this was not a job commensurate with his education. What made things even more confusing was that he was aware that upward social mobility and individual achievement were also highly valued goals in his subculture. One was accepted because he was Greek, but one was also expected to achieve because he was Greek. Bill's Greek peers had all gone to college and were highly successful in their different professions. Obviously, Bill could not relax in his current job. He was buffeted by conflicting expectations of how he should think and what he should do.What fueled this conflict, I thought, was the symbiotic relationship he had with his mother. Bill had clearly been the "man of the house" since his father's death when he was twelve years old. He lived with his mother in the house she grew up in, and she depended on him for a broad range of emotional needs. She cooked for him, they went to church together, he called when he expected to be out late, and he did the repairs on the house. Bill did have a girlfriend he had been seeing since his senior year in college, for three years at the time he came to me. This was a "full" relationship, Bill said, and the sexual part was "good." But his girlfriend Connie had never met his mother. He seemed bewildered that I was surprised by this; he never thought much about it, he said. His mother knew who Connie was and had never said anything disapproving about their relationship. Now that I forced him to think about it, he realized that he kept these two aspects of his life separate. It was clear to me, if not to Bill, that he and his mother had colluded in a covert agreement to make this woman Connie a nonperson who would not disrupt their mutually dependent relationship. It didn't surprise me that Connie wasn't Greek, since she was not considered to be a real marriage prospect. I knew that in Greek culture, non-Greek women were considered suspect and all Greek women by definition were acceptable. In this case, this was not an issue. Bill's mother recognized that he had sexual needs that had to be met outside the home, but she was determined to meet his emotional needs herself.

Bill had been doing Benson's Relaxation Response,[5] and I now introduced cognitive restructuring as a technique to counteract the ruminative thoughts that plagued him more persistently now. I had him close his eyes and think of an anxious thought related to his upcoming interview. We then replaced this thought with a "script" we had prepared to counteract the unrealistic, anxiety-generating ones he had associated with situations in which he would be judged. Bill took well to this cognitive restructuring. He practiced it systematically when he woke up in the morning as well as spontaneously in the course of the day.[6]

In our next session, Bill reported that he had done the relaxation response twice a day during the past week, which had a "somewhat" calming effect on him. He also monitored his behavior and noticed that he felt anxious whenever he thought of having a job interview. He felt a low level of anxiety "all the time," except when he was working or with Connie. He thought he was more tense when he was home with his mother, but he was not sure about this.

I decided to start a systematic "desensitization." This involved imagery training, in which Bill would imagine himself in an anxiety-provoking situation, picturing as many details as possible. He would then shut it off, following up with the relaxation response.[7] A week later Bill reported feeling much calmer, though he was still considerably apprehensive about his trip to the West Coast and the job interviews that awaited him there. I wondered out loud how much of his anxiety was caused by the anticipated interviews and how much by the separation he would have to experience in moving to another part of the country. He acknowledged that separations were always a problem for him. Going to camp and college had been traumatic, but he didn't think that was the major issue now, since he'd be with his family in California.

In our fourth session, Bill and I simulated a job interview in the context of a role-playing method. I took the role of interviewer and began to ask Bill questions. He became visibly anxious after the second question and said he couldn't continue. He said he felt like he was tied up and placed on railroad tracks and a train was approaching and he couldn't get free—as if he was in too far and was losing control. We stopped the "interview" and continued with the desensitization process. Within a few weeks Bill was more ready to take two job interviews he had set up in Boston. I decided to help him prepare by trying a "flooding" technique.[8] This involved his mentally constructing a high-anxiety job interview situation, making it as bad as possible with my verbal cues, and his mentally staying in the scene until his anxiety began to decrease. This took about ten minutes, after which I had him do the relaxation response.

After these simulated interviews, Bill described what happened. He had had some anxiety just before the interview, but after he had responded to the first question, his anxiety had disappeared entirely.

We talked about his trip to the West Coast. He was apprehensive about the move, but felt he could handle the job interviews. I was not as confident as Bill about this. I sensed his vulnerability and his reliance on his family for support. Bill lacked the confidence and self-assertion that is typical of Greek males who have been able to identify with their fathers. Bill thanked me, showing no signs of termination anxiety, and did not mention contacting me again.

About five weeks after our last session, Bill called me from the West Coast. He was returning to Boston and wanted to see me. He sounded distressed. When he appeared in my office, he looked tired. He told me that when he had found his family waiting for him around the dinner table at his sister's house, he experienced a panic he could not understand. He had drunk a lot that day and night. When his brother talked about the job interviews he had arranged for Bill, his anxiety rose, as did his alcohol consumption. Nevertheless, his interviews went well, and he took a job with a large food brokerage firm as a sales representative. But the first day on the job, he had a full-blown anxiety attack that started almost immediately after he arrived at the office. Somehow he got through the day, but he never went back.

His brother was really angry, as he had made the job contacts for him. His brother-in-law and sister were clearly disappointed but tried to be supportive. His mother called daily and expressed her worry about his anxiety, and said he was right to leave the job since it upset him so. Her response enraged him and made him feel even more helpless. He spent the next couple of weeks just hanging around his sister's house and drinking, and finally drove home alone across the country.

I listened to his story and offered my support. I contracted with him to resume doing the relaxation response, to stop drinking, and to reestablish social contacts in the Boston area—especially with Connie. He had not referred to her until I asked. He said that he had seen her since he returned and had slept at her apartment a couple of nights. He hadn't ended his relationship with her when he went west, and he had left the relationship as it always was—undefined. He had never said he would marry her, he told me, and she seemed to feel okay about their arrangement.

I resumed seeing Bill on a weekly basis. It would now be possible for me to complete the behavioral analysis and to set up some broader treatment goals. During this time our sessions focused on continuing the behavioral analysis and anxiety management. In our sessions Bill also focused a great deal on his mother. She had always been fearful of life, he said, and constantly warned him to be careful of getting hurt when he was growing up. She encouraged him to avoid confronting difficult situations, such as problems with peers or finishing a task he had started, like building a model plane. When he studied a great deal she worried that he would get too tired. After his father died, she became unbearably overprotective.

Bill's contact with his father had been minimal. His father had been part owner of a restaurant and had worked constantly. His parents did not get along well; he remembered being awakened at night by their arguing. His father drank a great deal, and Bill remembered hearing his mother accuse him of going out with other women. This had especially frightened him. Bill said little about his siblings, other than that they lived in different worlds. They cared about him, but he never really felt close to them. I knew that his mother's fearfulness about life was partially culturally patterned, as was her over-protectiveness. She had grown up in a rural area of Greece and had internalized an orientation to the physical and social environment that incorporated the belief that one is subject to the vagaries of life and vulnerable to forces beyond one's control. Her husband, Bill's father, had been unable to provide her with the sense of safety and love she needed. After his death, she turned to her children for support. She had no occupation, and depended on her children for emotional survival. In Greek families, the youngest child is often designated as the one to take care of the parents in old age or to care for the survivor if one parent dies. Bill was the one designated to provide her with what she needed, and she meant to see to it that she was not cut off.

These cultural insights helped me understand what Bill was up against. His "individuation" would have to almost literally be a life-and-death struggle. It also became evident that Bill faced issues of acculturation that paralleled those of his mother. He, too, was torn between two culturally patterned sets of expectations, Greek and American, and his individuation involved issues of culture change. Breaking the symbiotic bond with his mother meant differentiating between mutually contradictory expectations of how he should think, feel, and act. To his mother, being a good son meant living with her, spending time with her, and maintaining a primary emotional tie to her that excluded others. In return his mother provided a feeling of safety, shielding him from the anxiety incumbent in moving out to "American" ways in love and work. Thus when Bill moved toward assuming responsibility and behaving independently in the occupational area, he felt lonely and fearful that he couldn't accomplish his assigned tasks. These feelings were followed by the anxiety that he would be judged negatively by an employer and fired. The final abandonment—Bill's vulnerability to feelings of rejection by authority figures—was, of course, traceable to the absence of a father. He had not learned appropriate male role behaviors in the context of a traditional Greek family structure in which the father assumes the dominant role. Outside of work, commitment to a woman, especially a non-Greek woman, would mean a final emotional separation from his mother. He would be expected to perform, to take care of others, to be independent; he feared he would be found wanting and be cast out, and thus be abandoned again.

Individuation for Bill, then, essentially involved a culture change process. He needed to extinguish the anxiety he would feel by moving in "American" directions and to experience the reinforcing effects of thinking, feeling, and acting in "individualistic" ways. This is how I processed Bill's efforts to move out into an occupation at this juncture of treatment.

After two sessions, his anxiety had subsided significantly; at this point he had been in Boston for about three weeks. He drank only occasionally now, he said, and was ready to try again. In fact, he had located a possible job through a friend. I supported his determination to try again by pursuing an appropriate job. This was the obvious direction to go in furthering his individuation process. The major focus in this phase of treatment thus became the management of Bill's anxiety as he moved into the job market.

He made a job contact through a friend who was a buyer for a large department store chain. His friend suggested that Bill spend time with him during his work week to become familiar with what he did and to determine whether he wanted to apply for a job with the same company. This seemed to me an ideal arrangement in that it provided graduated exposure within the real work environment to the anxiety-evoking events or stimuli that Bill would need to confront in taking this job. Bill agreed.

The first day he accompanied his friend as he made the rounds of department stores. Though he was merely an observer, he became anxious anyway. He obsessed about the different operations involved in carrying out the job. He worried that he wouldn't be able to remember everything. He worried about the bosses he hadn't even met. Nevertheless, after two weeks of this "trial" period, Bill decided to apply for a job as a buyer. His anxiety shot up the minute his friend agreed to set up an interview with the regional manager.

As the day for the job interview approached, Bill's anxiety increased. I suggested he practice the flooding technique he had learned earlier, which he did. On the day of the interview, he was very anxious. He felt panic driving to the interview—"Like I was going to be executed," he said. During the interview itself, however, he relaxed after a few moments, and the rest of the half hour was uneventful. He was offered the job, and a starting date was set for approximately six weeks later.

During that period, Bill's anxiety varied widely in intensity, but it was now clear to me that the anxiety management techniques were not having the enduring effect that I expected. He reported dreams of being pursued because he had murdered someone and felt, he said, as if he was holding a hand grenade from which the pin had been pulled. He began drinking heavily again. Benson's Relaxation Response, he said, was not enough. The cognitive restructuring seemed hardly worth doing.

It gradually became clearer to me that the approaching starting date for his new job was not the main source of Bill's anxiety. It merely provided the context for a counterforce to his moving out that his mother, first subtly but now obviously, had presented. I had underestimated this effect and until now had not seen that Bill was in fact not in a position "developmentally" to take on the responsibilities that a job like this would demand of him. He had missed earlier individuation steps, or stages of separation from his mother, that would have to be traversed before he could successfully undertake such a job.

Bill's mother announced a week before he was to start his new job that she was taking a two-week vacation. His anxiety level increased markedly. Then he got a call from the regional office asking him whether he would be willing to relocate to another part of the country, should this be necessary. He became anxious all the time. None of the behavioral techniques worked, he said. He drank more.

He showed up for the first day of work and managed somehow to get through it. I saw him three times that week. He felt better after each session, but his high anxiety level was not appreciably reduced. He lasted another week on the job. The following week I received a call from his mother, who had just returned from vacation. She told me Bill had been hospitalized for an acute intestinal problem complicated by excessive drinking. He remained in the hospital for three days and returned home to recuperate for an additional ten days. When he came for his next session he was haggard and worn.

He told me that he was drinking all day in order to block out his anxiety. When his mother had returned from her trip, he threw himself into her arms and cried. She encouraged him not to return to work. She was, he said, devastated by his drinking because it brought back memories of her husband's alcoholism.

Bill called his employer to say he had to take an indefinite leave of absence because of illness. He spent his time at home with his mother, feeling more helpless and more powerless than ever before in his life. Whenever he thought of finding employment of any kind, he became anxious. During the second week after his discharge from the hospital, he only left his house for his appointments with me. I saw him twice a week for the next four weeks.

My immediate goal was to help him reduce his feelings of helplessness. My support took the form of listening, empathizing, and providing him with alternative cognitive modes of processing his feelings of being overwhelmed. I made these cognitive inputs by citing examples of the helplessness some of my other patients have felt, followed by suggesting a solution to his immediate problem of employment: He looked surprised when I suggested that he return to work at his uncle's restaurant. "Wasn't the whole idea to move away from the protective environment of the family business?" he wondered out loud.

I told him that moving back into a Greek environment was a kind of behavioral counterpart to the psychoanalytic concept of "regression in the service of the ego." Bill could be expected to relax in this environment and to be strengthened by the unconditional support he could expect to receive from his uncle and coworkers at the restaurant. He had often expressed to me the notion that in non-Greek working situations, people were highly competitive and would just as soon "chew you up and spit you out." In other words, he experienced the competitiveness of coworkers as a personal threat. He experienced the "American" workplace this way because he was socialized in a subculture where mutual support and caring are highly valued behaviors. One is first judged by who one "is," and second by what one does. Bill also needed to feel effective at this point, to engage in work that he knew how to do and that would produce steady approval and satisfaction. I envisioned his next step as taking a job in the broader "American" marketplace, but he obviously was not ready for this at the time. He also needed help to separate himself emotionally and gradually from his symbiotic relationship with his mother. This process would include his learning to relate in more adult ways to women. This whole thrust in the treatment needed to be undertaken gradually, however, as Bill became stabilized emotionally by working in an environment where the probability of success was high and where he could be sure to be accepted and supported. This strategy was remarkably effective. During the next six months I saw Bill once a week, and he stabilized emotionally. The anticipated effects of his work environment were also realized. He brought his anxiety under control, his depression lifted, and his self-esteem was restored.

When Bill told his mother that he was going back to work at his uncle's restaurant, she expressed her disappointment. She had hoped, she said, that he would accomplish more in life than being a waiter. He was feeling more angry at her now than he could ever remember feeling before; he could almost believe, he said, that she didn't want him to get better. He related a dream he had repeatedly of his mother dying. He took up with me his reactivated doubts about going to work at the restaurant; I reminded him that this was a transitional step and he could later move in other directions when it became clearer what he wanted to do.

His work situation over the next six months gave Bill the opportunity to make gains in two important areas. The first was his anxiety about being judged by authority figures; the second was his anxiety about exerting his authority over subordinates. These were obviously two aspects of the same issue.

He identified his anger and the anxiety it activated when his uncle treated him arbitrarily. Bill was not "Greek" enough to be able to accept his uncle's prerogative to dominate those below him in the restaurant hierarchy, and he also was not "American" enough to be able to assert his rights as an individual in a democratic system. His confusion left him feeling helpless and enraged. I pointed out the above cultural distinction to him, and we then rehearsed ways that he could assert himself with his uncle without violating the uncle's dignity as the dominant "boss." Essentially, Bill stood up to him, forcefully asserting his position while at the same time openly expressing his respect. He chose appropriate times to do this, when other workers were not around. His uncle got the message; he began to treat Bill with more respect and assigned him greater responsibilities in managing the large number of waiters and waitresses.

The behavioral rehearsal we did in relation to his uncle affected his ability to supervise the work of the waiters and waitresses. They gradually began to treat him with more respect after he successfully handled two or three difficult incidents. They had challenged his authority, but he stood his ground firmly and without anger, and they eventually came around.

These experiences reinforced Bill's general sense of control over his environment. He now began to stand up more to his mother. He refused to tell her of his whereabouts when he stayed out late and was not as available to her to do chores. She began to develop psychosomatic complaints.

Bill began to spend less and less time at home, which was especially upsetting to his mother. It had become clearer to me after Bill started working again at his uncle's restaurant that his lifestyle was impoverished. He essentially worked from late afternoon until early morning, slept until midmorning, and then spent the intervening leisure time reading books in his room or interacting with his mother, usually about chores that needed to be done. He saw Connie on his day off and occasionally stayed overnight at her apartment. They sometimes went to a show together. He continued to make very little of this relationship in our sessions. I decided to wait before focusing on it until I felt he was well stabilized himself. At this point, I introduced a new and perplexing concept for Bill—that gratifications were an important ingredient of mental health. It was crucial for him at this time to explore ways he could increase the frequency of experiences outside of work that gave him pleasure. I said I was not referring to sensual pleasure as such, but rather to the broader range of experiences that resulted in a sense of well-being. Usually these involved interactions in which he could feel effective.

It was not easy to get this concept across. Bill's notion of pleasure based on Greek value orientations was clearly a "being" one. One got pleasure exclusively by resting physically, by being nourished through food and drink, and by being satisfied sexually by a woman. The more American "doing" orientation as a source of pleasure was foreign to him. He engaged in sports only rarely and had few interests outside of working, except for reading. I asked him first to monitor his daily activities for a week; he was surprised at how little he did outside of work and being with his mother. We then reviewed the full range of possibilities and actually programmed an alternative lifestyle for him. He started jogging daily after getting up. He registered for accounting courses at a college, which he thought might be helpful for the career he would later pursue. He contacted some male friends he hadn't seen for a while and arranged to play softball on Saturday mornings. He even developed a latent interest in fishing.

This lifestyle restructuring effort was accomplished over several weeks. He felt markedly better; his anxiety level decreased.

This effort also brought into sharper relief for him his dependency on his mother. He was, of course, always aware of it, but now his own collusion in his dependency became more apparent to him. As he moved away from her she intensified her efforts to draw him back. He was better able to handle his own anxiety about this progressive separation from her because of the reinforcing aspects of his new lifestyle. Bill's Americanization was also, in effect, his course for individuation.

Bill also transferred a good deal of his dependent needs to me, a problem of transference. In the end he separated from me in the same way he was now doing from his mother, by interacting with his environment in a way that assured that his needs for intimacy were appropriately gratified. As he moved away from his mother, Bill also became aware of her irrational fears. Her experience of the world as unmanageable and threatening was, he could now see, mirrored in his own perceptions. When he observed himself making statements that reflected her feelings of helplessness and vulnerability, he was now better able to replace these statements with more rational ones.

Bill continued to do the relaxation response twice a day during this period, and he used the flooding technique whenever he was unable to handle anxiety-evoking interactions appropriately. Simply put, Bill had learned how to manage stress.

A year after my initial contact with Bill he was stabilized; his anxiety was under control for the first time. Our therapeutic alliance was consolidated. However, in the spheres of love and work, a great deal remained to be done.

I saw Bill once a week over the next nine months, and then once a month for seven months. He made rapid progress in the spheres of love and work. I suggested he broaden his experience with women by dating more and contracted with him to make specific moves when his resistance hampered him. He had a relationship with another woman, which helped him work through many dependency issues, as well as his feelings of being trapped.

Eventually he broke off with this woman and tried to start up again with Connie, who agreed to date him only reluctantly.

During this time, Bill also started reading want ads again, which caused him some anxiety. As the day approached for his interview for a management training program of a major hotel chain, I suggested that he do the flooding exercise he had learned earlier. He did these exercises several times a week for two weeks preceding his interview, and was subsequently accepted into the program. His new tasks generated anxiety, but he confronted it and coped effectively in the end.

Throughout these events, he was able to employ the techniques for managing his anxiety that he had previously learned in our sessions. I also reinforced him continually for his successes and taught him to accept his failures. He regressed from time to time and, in fact, reverted to drinking too much on at least three occasions, although only for short periods. We began a gradual termination period, during which Bill felt no need to verbalize his feelings about me. I understood that he felt strong positive feelings toward me of the kind that Greek men do not express directly to each other. By the time we terminated his treatment, Bill was ensconced in a satisfying job and was preparing to get married—to Connie. He could now be a father in his own home.

NOTES

1. J. Papajohn & J. P. Spiegel, *Transactions in families: A modern approach for resolving cultural and generational conflicts*, chap. 6 (San Francisco: Jossey-Bass, 1975), pp. 179–206.

2. A. Scourby, *The Greek Americans* (Boston: Twayne, 1984).

3. C. C. Moskos, *Greek Americans: Struggle and success*, 2nd ed. (Englewood Cliffs, NJ: Prentice Hall, 1989).

4. J. Papajohn & J. P. Spiegel, The relationship of cultural value orientation change and Rorschach indices of psychological development, *Journal of Cross-Cultural Psychology* 2(3) (1971), 257–272.

5. H. Benson, *The relaxation response* (New York: Avon Books, 1975).

6. A. Beck, *Cognitive therapy and emotional disorders* (New York: International Universities Press, 1976).

7. J. Wolpe, *Psychotherapy by reciprocal inhibition* (Stanford: Stanford University Press, 1958).

8. T. Stamphl & D. Levis, Essentials of implosive therapy: A learning theory based on psychodynamic behavioral therapy, *Journal of Abnormal Psychology 72* (1967), 496–503.

AN ITALIAN-WASP MARRIAGE

MARIANNE JONES AND TONY PHILLIPS

Marianne and Tony met during their freshman year at the college they attended in their hometown. The mutual attraction was strong and endured the rest of their four years there. Married shortly after they graduated, they had much earlier agreed to leave the small Midwestern town where they were born and move to Boston to pursue their careers.

Marianne is of northern European extraction, a mixture of Scottish and Irish stock. Her ancestors had emigrated to the United States some time in the middle 1800s. Her family was typically Midwestern, middle class, and Protestant, and had mainstream American values. Her father, a college graduate, held a lower level managerial position in a large national company. Her mother, who had finished high school in the town where Marianne grew up, did not hold a job outside her home. Marianne was an only child.

Both of Tony's parents were Italian-American. His grandparents on both sides were born in Italy; his parents, who were born in the United States, met and married in New York State. Tony's father, a high school graduate, was a welder by trade. He had moved with his wife and two children to the Midwest when he was offered a good job there shortly after World War II. He was now in his early seventies and in poor health; some four years earlier, he had been diagnosed with cancer, which had been in remission but was showing signs of recurring.

Marianne and Tony's move to the Boston area was problematic from the start. She had gotten an excellent job in a large corporation and was advancing up the corporate ladder. Determined to succeed, she put a great deal of her energy into her work and had no problem with the long hours of work and the travel that effort demanded.

Tony also had gotten a good job in a small firm, where he wrote technical descriptions of products manufactured by different companies in the computer industry. He worked at home, enjoyed it, and was compensated well.

In spite of their mutual professional successes, however, after only two years of marriage, Marianne and Tony were deeply disappointed in each other. Their marriage was coming apart, and they decided to seek professional help in the hope of salvaging it. Neither of them, however, had much confidence that this would happen, but they felt they ought to give marital therapy a try as a last-ditch effort.

When they presented themselves in my office, I was impressed by the intelligent and articulate way they explained their problem. Marianne is a tall, thin, attractive woman, with blond hair and blue eyes. She was dressed in a well-tailored pin-striped business suit. Tony was more casually dressed. He is a tall, dark-complected man with sharply defined facial features and an athletic build. They immediately inquired into my credentials and wanted to know what my "success rate" was in marital therapy.

Marianne started off by complaining bitterly about her husband's constant complaint that he felt socially isolated in Boston. He missed his friends back home and was preoccupied with his parents' issues: he had a recently divorced sister who had moved back in with her parents. The sister was very dependent, and her problems further stressed his parents, who were already dealing with his father's poor health. Marianne said also that Tony was not at all emotionally supportive of her and that she had no one to talk to about her work and the stresses she had to deal with there. She resented Tony's demanding her support around his father's illness when he had behaved so callously and insensitively to her own father's death a year earlier. Her rage became visible as she recalled how he had openly expressed his resentment at her frequent visits home toward the end of her father's life. Tony listened patiently, and I sensed a condescending tone in his voice as he rebutted her complaints. He was, he said, sorry for not being more supportive during her father's illness. As he talked I revised my earlier impression that he was condescending, as he now seemed sincere in expressing his regret. He quickly moved, however, to a counterattack. His wife, he said, is never available to him in the normal course of the week. They don't eat breakfast together because she leaves for work very early in the morning. She often works late, and it's not unusual for her to arrive home at ten at night, having had dinner with her business associates. Even on those days when she gets home "early"—that is, around seven o'clock—she is so exhausted that their meal together had become her time to unload her work stresses on him. On weekends, when she isn't away on business trips, she is too tired to socialize.

While at college, Tony had worked to free himself from the strong pull of the neediness that characterized his family's relationships. He had succeeded at this, but at a price. Tony chose not to live at home, even though his college was in the same town, and worked extra jobs to be able to afford it. During his first year at college, he was constantly anxious; he had never been so far from home emotionally before. He endured this anxiety without really understanding its source and managed to reduce it by bonding closely with new friends at college. He had developed many relationships with men and dated Marianne regularly. In essence, Tony had developed a surrogate extended family, without conceptualizing it or consciously intending it. This "family" gave him a ready source of emotional support.

Tony had initially been attracted to Marianne because of her independence and strong drive for individual achievement. His attraction to her was in part a reaction to his own family's inter-dependence. He was also drawn to her, on the other hand, be-cause she embodied those American values that, cognitively at least, he identified himself with. This discrepancy was well be-yond his awareness; at that time he was totally unable to under-stand the inconsistency. To Tony, the notion that he was in a situation of culture conflict was at best incomprehensible, if not totally irrelevant. Nevertheless, this conflict was present in his marriage, as evidenced in the deep negative emotions that were dividing Tony and Marianne.

Marianne had gotten the wrong messages from her husband-to-be. She believed that he accepted, in fact that he would vali-date, her strong drive to succeed professionally. She had made it clear to him during their long courtship that she did not want to have babies because they would interfere with her career. He had readily agreed. What further evidence did she need that Tony understood her aims and intentions, her value orienta-tions? She thought their marriage was based on a mutually ac-cepted vision of what direction their life together would take, of what was important to both of them. So did Tony, but they were both obviously wrong.

While Tony had not married an Italian wife, his unconscious expectations of an intimate relationship were based on his expe-rience in his Italian family. He expected the kind of closeness that Marianne was not socialized to provide. She valued her space and was intent on having it. Her major sense of well-being derived from her capacity to cope, to solve problems in her job, to get things done. Her leisure time was a chance to recharge her batteries. For Marianne, feeling emotional closeness to her husband was a way to become revitalized, "re-created"—but not an end in itself. When emotional closeness became an end in itself, when it became the primary source of feeling good, it left her feeling weak, disempowered, and dependent—and thus usually made her angry.

For Tony, on the other hand, the relationship of work to pleasure was a mixed bag. Yes, he enjoyed his work, but to him work was something you did because you had to, to survive. To Tony, when the day's work was done, it was time to really start living, to get pleasure from all available sources—food, sex, and primarily close personal relationships. The sheer joy of being with family and friends was what it was all about for him, was where he could be totally himself, spontaneously expressing whatever feelings he was having.

Tony didn't express his complaints to Marianne in quite these terms, but the message was there and easy for me to interpret from what he was describing, though I didn't express this at the time. My interpretation was based on my understanding of American mainstream and Italian value orientations. The profiles characterizing these two cultures are reproduced in Table 2.

The discrepancy between American and Italian value orientations in the *relational* area is reflected in Marianne and Tony's difficulties. Her behavior is consistent with a preference for Individualism in the first-order position, while his is consistent with a first-order Collateral (Interdependent) orientation.

This first-order interdependency orientation is also reflected in Tony's strong loyalty to his family. In the month before Tony called me, his father's health had begun to deteriorate. He had to be hospitalized for more chemotherapy, after which his doctors recommended that he be placed in a nursing home. He was obviously terminal. His wife and daughter would not hear of putting him in a nursing home; instead they transformed their living room into a hospital room and brought him home, where they tended to his needs. Tony's mother called and asked Tony to come home to help them cope with the crisis, and even suggested that they transport his father by ambulance to Boston so Tony could take care of him there.

Marianne was shocked by this suggestion. She thought it was totally inappropriate and said as much to her husband. While Tony agreed that transporting his father to Boston was impractical, he also experienced Marianne's attitude as further evidence of her incapacity to be empathic and loving. It confirmed his gradually developing perception of her as "evil." His view of human nature was more Italian than American (see *human nature* dimension in Table 1): one is either evil or good. The couple argued and finally agreed that Tony would fly home for long weekends to help his mother and sister care for his father and to give them emotional support.

By the end of our initial session, I had already begun an intervention that can be technically termed "cognitive-restructuring." I addressed directly their differing ways of processing the same events and traced this back to the value orientations that each of them had internalized in their early socialization process in their respective homes. I set the stage, at an intellectual level, to make it possible for each of them to understand more objectively that their different ways of thinking, feeling, and acting were due to their different value orientations and that this was affecting their ability to have an intimate relationship.

They caught on fast, and their new insights—or rather "broadsights"—into what had gone wrong somewhat eased the rage that had pulled them apart. Tony was able to see that Marianne's stance in terms of both her work and her relationship with him was not based on her flawed character but on her values, which he also shared in part. Marianne was able to see that Tony's posture toward his family was not based on a pathological codependency, but on an ethnically patterned belief of what was required in such situations. The pressure was markedly relieved. Marianne now could accompany her husband on his visits home and "tune in" to what was expected of her there without feeling that her personal dignity was being violated.

My therapeutic intervention also included a second critical dimension, which can be termed "behavioral." I directly addressed their lifestyle and suggested ways they could modify it to increase the amount of time they spent together and to enhance the quality of that time. We examined their weekly schedules and found ways to rearrange them so they could have more meals and more relaxed leisure time together. Tony was delighted that Marianne would agree to be home by six on designated days of the week and stopped hassling her when she needed to work late. These rearrangements were brought about through "contracting" with the therapist to effect the mutually agreed on changes. At the beginning of each therapy session I reviewed the previous week's "contract" to determine whether it had been carried out. They both allowed me to help them negotiate these basic changes in the structure of their marriage. It was the easing of their anger toward each other, however, through the clarification of their frustrated expectations of each other based on their discrepant values, that made these behavioral and "structural" changes possible.

We also addressed their meager sex life. Frequency had dropped to zero; they hadn't made love in more than six months. I reviewed with them Masters and Johnson's[1] principles for sexual retraining, which involves a gradual, step-wise reinstigation of sexual behavior. They were instructed to initially be in bed together, unclothed, and to allow sufficient time—several nights—to enjoy each other's close physical proximity without any intimate contact. When they had become de-sensitized to any negative feeling of being close physically, they were to start phase two—the sensory focusing stage. In this second stage, lasting from one to several nights, they were instructed to touch each other—though not in erogenous zones—and to give each other pleasure through massaging each other, using creams or oils if they desired. The third stage involved stimulating each other in erogenous zones but not having intercourse. The next stage involved partial intercourse, and in the last stage, of course, full intercourse was completed. This graded approach, which Tony and Marianne took to well, enabled them to resume having sex twice a week.

We were about three months into weekly therapy when they called to tell me that Tony's father had died. A week after the funeral, they returned to Boston and we met to resume treatment.

Tony reported that Marianne had been very supportive to him, as well as to his mother and sister, throughout the ordeal. In fact, the tragedy had drawn them closer together. Tony's mother, surprisingly, also drew closer to Marianne, although they had never really gotten along well in the past (Could an Italian mother forgive her daughter-in-law for not having children?)

We only needed to meet three more times. We focused next on expanding their social life. They began to invite friends for dinner and found other ways to broaden their social contacts. Tony stopped feeling the need to relocate back to their hometown. I called them a few months after we terminated treatment. Marianne laughed when she announced that she was pregnant.

NOTE

1. W. H. Mastern & V. E. Johnson, *Human sexual inadequacy* (Boston, MA: Little, Brown & Co., 1970).

7

A GREEK-IRISH MARRIAGE

BRIGITTE AND
GEORGE CONSTANTINE

Brigitte and George Constantine were being seen in couples therapy by a colleague of mine, who decided that George needed a therapist of his own. She felt he needed support, since at times he became passive and withdrawn during their combined sessions, usually in response to the frequent angry assaults his wife made on him. He was quite angry at her but could not express it. Instead he remained externally calm and rational, which infuriated his wife even more.

In his initial session with me, George spoke in the calm, rational manner my colleague had described. He is sixty-one years old, has a dark, swarthy complexion, and is somewhat overweight. A successful restaurateur/businessman, he has been married to Brigitte for thirty-five years. George is a high school graduate; he has two sisters who are partners in his family restaurant business.

George's newlywed parents had emigrated from a village in southern Greece in the early 1900s. Brigitte's grandparents emigrated from Ireland in the late 1800s. Her parents were born in the Boston area. She also is a high school graduate and has several brothers and sisters, who all live in the Boston area. She married George when she was twenty-two and he was twenty-five. They have two daughters and a son, all college graduates doing well in their respective professions.

Their trouble began, George told me, about three years earlier when their last child had finished college and announced that she wanted to marry a classmate of hers. They had met the young man and both apparently approved of him. Shortly after their daughter's announcement, however, Brigitte began to become progressively more agitated. She said that their daughter's intended marriage had aroused feelings about her own marriage to George, which at that time she had been able to suppress. Essentially, she was enraged at the way George's family had treated her over the years. She realized that they had never really accepted her, she said, because she was not Greek. In their relationship, his family always came first when decisions needed to be made in a wide range of situations: at whose home they would celebrate different holidays, when George could take a vacation from the restaurant, the salaries to be paid to their children when they worked there on weekends and during summer vacations. George always deferred to his sisters. His sisters' children got preferential treatment in terms of work schedules and were always overpaid. It was also clear to Brigitte that George always considered his mother and father's needs before hers. She had been a dutiful wife and put up with all of this over the years, and now she was finally able to feel it all. On top of this, she said George never sided with her when an argument arose between her and their friends.

George remained calm as he described his "wife's problem"— and he made it clear that this was her problem. She was demented, overreacting to life events, and not open to reason. His desperation, however, was evident despite his outward calm.

My first effort involved empathizing with George's distress, while at the same time attempting to help him understand that the issues between him and Brigitte involved an interaction and could not be explained solely on the basis of her craziness. I wondered how supportive he had been of her while their children were growing up. In Greek families, men are expected to work hard and to support the family well but not to be involved in child rearing or to be responsive to their wives' stresses in the domestic sphere of their lives. Greek men are also socialized to maintain strong emotional ties to their parents and siblings throughout their lives. They feel obligated to do this, and at times these commitments compete with their strong commitments to their own children. It is an apparent paradox that Greek men can attain a high degree of individualism in their lives, while remaining respectful sons. Greek men do not individuate by rebelling against their fathers during adolescence. Instead, the son accepts and respects his father's authoritarian role. In return for accepting his father's position as head of the household, the son receives his father's unwavering support—emotional, financial, and other, with basically no limits. The son's own independence is attained by modeling, that is, by identifying with the father's strength. In "healthy" Greek families, love and respect toward the father become indistinguishable. While George was not born in Greece, he was socialized in a Greek family and had internalized these value orientations.

George flatly denied the relevance of any interpretations I made that were based on "cultural" considerations. His wife, he responded, was as crazy as her mother. He compared his mother-in-law's irrationality to his wife's, graphically describing her behavior over the years.

George began to become exasperated with me over the next few sessions, and I was not getting anywhere with him. He had fixed on a biological understanding of his wife's anger and was not buying any psychological interpretations, much less cultural ones. I had overestimated George's internalization of American values. He was not able to conceptualize psychologically, despite his high intelligence. The absence of psychological causality from the worldview of Greeks was well known to me, but I had been misled by George's apparent Americanization.

In a compulsive manner, he now repeatedly came back to his genetic understanding of Brigitte's problem. He felt she was sick and needed medicine to get well. Period.

It was clear that I needed to shift tactics and move myself in a more culturally enlightened manner. I suggested that George ask his wife to come with him to the following session.

Brigitte is an attractive woman with strawberry blond hair, overweight, who made no effort to disguise her anger as she sat next to her husband on the couch in my office. She informed me from the outset that it was clear to her that her husband was not making much progress in his sessions with me. She was sure, she said, that I was taken in by his calm, benign manner and that he had convinced me she was the problem. I needed to gain her confidence if I was to get anywhere in this conjoint session. I told her that her husband was very distressed by their marital conflict and was committed to her and their marriage. This statement had the opposite effect of what I had intended. She became visibly more agitated, her face flushed, and she let go a stream of invective toward her husband that I worried could end in a physical assault. His insensitivity to her emotional needs over the years was the major theme, and she documented this with numerous examples of his callousness toward her, including events that had occurred in the last two weeks. She could not remain seated and got up from the couch, pacing back and forth. Her husband remained calm and impassive.

In Irish families, which are matriarchal in their structure, it is critically important for women to maintain a strong position not only in relation to their children but toward their husbands as well. This is the exact opposite of Greek families, in which the father is expected to maintain a dominant, authoritarian position in relation to his wife and children. Brigitte and George had been locked in a power struggle for most of their married lives with little, if any, conscious awareness of the fact. This struggle was played out in a variety of ways, which on the surface appeared to be the usual struggles of couples; that is, the problems of living, conflicts with relatives, friends, children, and so on. In fact, these conflicts constituted only the content of the culturally patterned roles of husband and wife that for George and Brigitte were fixed by their disparate ethnic traditions.

Their power struggle was being played out in an interesting way. George reported that Brigitte would begin her verbal assault on him every day the minute he came home. As he described it, this verbal barrage had an obsessive quality to it. Brigitte would regale him with accusations of his uncaring, nonempathic stance toward her in a wide range of situations, from the past up to the present—for example, he had not sided with her when she got into an argument with friends the night before. Family events gave her the ideal opportunity to bring up slights in years past involving interaction with his sisters.

George dealt with these assaults by attempting to reason with his wife in his usual calm manner. This, of course, infuriated her more and energized her for the next round of invective. I had suggested to George in our individual sessions that he not respond to his wife in the manner described above, but that instead he leave the room until she had quieted down. This would discourage the obsessive, ruminative quality of her verbal attacks, which were causing her a great deal of distress and suffering. He had a better chance of reasoning with her when her obsessiveness had diminished. George agreed that he was fueling his wife's verbal attacks but refused to follow my suggestions about how to deal with it. It became clear he wanted her to suffer because of the suffering she was inflicting on him.

I developed an intervention strategy based on the above considerations and on the following. The fear of abandonment is employed freely by parents in Greek families to control their children's behavior. Parental love and caring, therefore, is conditional on the children's obedience and good behavior. Any behavior that can bring shame on the family is not tolerated. George's tolerance of his wife's hostility, which he believed was without merit, was based on the fact that divorce would constitute a far greater danger—a threat to the integrity of the family, as well as a catastrophic threat to his own emotional survival. I also sensed that Brigitte knew this and that it allowed her to "act out" her rage without fearing that her husband would leave her.

I suggested that I see George alone in the next session. I reviewed with him the fact that our sessions were not having a positive effect on his marriage. In addition, their relationship was being weakened further by the vicious battles they were having daily. What made sense, I said, was a trial separation to allow things to cool down between them.

George was visibly shaken by this suggestion. He attempted to discard the idea by saying his wife would never agree to it. We left it that he would discuss it with her. He left the office quite agitated.

The next day I received a call from Brigitte, who asked for an appointment for herself. There was a marked change in her demeanor. She was much more subdued and conciliatory. She wanted to know what purpose would be served by their separating. I repeated what I had told George. She listened and expressed doubt that this tactic could help. I guessed that separation would remove her from the arena where she could exert her power over her husband. In the end, however, she agreed to go along with my suggestion.

About an hour after she left my office, George called me. He was in a panic. Brigitte had announced that she agreed with me and that George should leave the house as soon as possible. He had left the house and was staying with his sister in the next town.

I agreed to see him the next day. His demeanor was also markedly altered. His self-assured, impatient posture had disappeared. He was visibly anxious but finally willing to entertain his possible role in his wife's anger toward him.

I saw him three times a week for the next month. He was in crisis, unable to work or to relate to anyone except his sister. He did not want to be considered vulnerable by any other family members. He had to maintain the strong patriarchal image that had characterized him. He also raised the question of anti-anxiety medication.

In the course of the next four weeks, George was gradually able to modify his perspective by considering his wife's complaints in a more empathic light. He could now see that her pain was based on the fact that he had in fact not been supportive of her in ways she had a right to expect. He became aware that his commitment to his parents and siblings took precedence over that to his wife. This could not be tolerated by most women in this society, much less by one of Irish extraction. He came to see that his wife needed to assert herself as a person and that her frustration and anger was based on her inability to do this within the framework of their marriage.

These insights calmed him considerably. He now felt less helpless, because it became clear to him what he needed to do to solve their marital problem.

He had been calling his wife regularly during this period, trying to placate her in patronizing ways. This had only enraged her more. Now he reached out to her in genuinely conciliatory ways. He expressed his regret that he had not been more empathic over the years. At first Brigitte was sure all this was a ploy to get her back, and she would have none of it. She, too, felt lonely and wanted to reconcile, but her distrust was too entrenched. Gradually, however, and over a protracted period in which George called every day, she relented provisionally. She agreed to allow George to return home with the condition that their reconciliation be contingent on their working out their differences. If after a reasonable period of time they could not do this, she would file for divorce. George of course agreed, confident now that they would work things out.

He terminated his sessions with me and agreed to call me in three months to let me know how things were going. When he didn't call, I called him.

His wife, he said, at first was quite tentative and distant in her relationship to him. She was testing him in every way, especially by continually exploding with anger at the slightest provocation. Now George reacted with genuine empathy rather than distancing himself as he had before. He had also modified his behavior toward his aging parents. He remained supportive, but validated his wife whenever it was appropriate. Brigitte took all of this in but didn't expect it to last.

I called again six months later. While they continued to have their ups and downs, their relationship was markedly improved. Brigitte still maintained a cautious stance, but her rages had disappeared. It would take some time, George said, but he felt confident that they would be okay.

8

A JEWISH-WASP MARRIAGE

JOAN AND DAVID SIEGEL

Joan Siegel sounded quite agitated over the phone. I assumed she was experiencing a recurrence of the anxiety attacks I had treated her for years before. She must have sensed this assumption, for she told me that she was doing fine but that her marriage was not. Her husband David, she said, was getting on her nerves to the point where she was considering separating from him. He was an attorney who practiced from an office that was attached to their home in a suburb of Boston. He had worked for several years in a prestigious law firm in Boston but had tired of the long hours and the unrelenting pressure to generate "billable hours." Although he was on the verge of becoming a partner in this firm, he decided it wasn't worth it and resigned. He decided to open his own office, taking some of his clients with him. In order to reduce overhead, he converted what was originally a barn on their property to law offices.

This was when the trouble began. He was always around, Joan complained to me in the initial session when I saw her alone in my office. Since his practice was now limited to a small number of clients, she found that he was following her around throughout the day, wanting her attention, expecting to have lunch with her, etc. This "dependency," as she termed it, had lowered her respect for him. He was behaving like an adolescent, and the stress was sapping her energies to the point of exhaustion. Furthermore, she had for years endured the intrusion of his family into their life. Although his father, also an attorney, lived in New York City, her husband constantly consulted him on professional matters. His mother visited them several times a year and stayed for as long as two weeks at a time. On Jewish holidays the entire clan descended upon Joan and David, including David's brother and sister, who were also attorneys. Joan was required to prepare the meals and entertain them. She described feeling engulfed—"asphyxiated"—by David's family, and now this new development of having him around constantly was more than she could bear.

David grew up in a suburb of New York City in an affluent upper-middle-class Jewish family that closely identified with Judaism. They supported the local temple, and Mrs. Siegel had served for a time as president of Hadassah, the Jewish women's organization. David and his siblings had attended private schools; David was a graduate of Columbia College and Harvard Law School. The Siegels had assumed that their children would find Jewish mates, which David's brother and sister in fact did. While at Harvard Law School, David had also dated Jewish women and had met Joan inadvertently. She was a nurse in the office of a physician he had consulted when he had a serious case of the flu. He had been very shy about approaching her, but finally mustered the courage to do so. David fell in love and pursued Joan persistently; a year later they were engaged.

It was during this period that I had originally seen Joan for an anxiety disorder that was brought on by the stress of her relationship with David. As she explained, she came from a totally different background than this man who wanted so desperately to marry her. She was born in Surrey, a county just south of London, toward the end of World War II. Her father, an officer in the Royal Air Force, was killed in the Battle of Britain. Her mother, whose family was wealthy, never remarried, and Joan was raised as an only child by her grandparents. She emigrated to Boston alone at the age of twenty-two when she enrolled in the nursing program at Boston University. She was baptized an Episcopalian but had never been a practicing Christian. She had known very few Jewish people while growing up and didn't know that her roommate, whom she had met through mutual friends, was Jewish until they had lived together for several months.

It was while they were making wedding plans that David raised the question of religion. It was then that Joan began to consider the implications of marrying someone Jewish. David wanted her to convert to Judaism. At first she readily consented, since he assured her that this required no commitment from her and it would greatly appease his parents. Furthermore, her ties to Christianity were quite weak. Gradually, however, the issue of her conversion began to weigh heavily upon her, more on psychological than on religious grounds. She felt that this demand was an encroachment on her personal identity, that it violated her sense of individualism. We addressed her anxious feelings in therapy, and Joan seemed to have worked them out. Her anxiety had subsided considerably, and at the time we terminated treatment she was much more relaxed and went on preparing for her marriage. This included going through a conversion ceremony preceded by instruction by a rabbi in a local temple.

I did not hear from her for several years. Joan now brought me up to date, telling me she had borne two children, both boys, and had been relatively content in her marriage until David moved his practice to their home. In the second session, Joan related another event that proved critical in their marital difficulties. Their children had reached school age—one son, age ten, was in the fifth grade, and the other, age nine, was in the fourth. David announced that he wanted them to attend Hebrew classes at the local temple in order to prepare for their bar mitzvahs. In order to do this, they were required to become members of the temple. Joan's long-repressed anger at David for persuading her to convert broke through. She adamantly refused to go along with David's desires. She also promptly began attending an Episcopal church in their town. David was disheartened by this "betrayal." He had never coerced her to convert, he said; she had consented being fully aware of what she was doing.

It soon became evident to me that the issue that was dividing this couple was not a religious one. I had been this woman's therapist, and I knew her to be as nonprejudiced as any person could hope to be. I also knew she was capable of deep commitment and that she wanted to preserve her marriage. I felt the conflict was basically cultural. I knew that Jewish-American families were characterized by strong, interdependent ties, which some describe as "enmeshment." Boundaries between the generations are permeable, parents remain significantly involved with their children throughout their lives, and children are supported emotionally to the point where they are seen by outsiders as overindulged. The negative "Jewish princess" designation derives from this perception. Paradoxically, however, Jewish children are also socialized for individual achievement in mainstream American terms. They are expected to excel in school and to develop into effective, independent individuals. It seems that whatever "codependency" is fostered in their formative years is offset by the strong drive for individual success, which is also strongly encouraged. These conflicting demands—for interdependence on the one hand and independence on the other—are often reconciled at the high cost of neurotic formations or worse.

I interpreted Joan's description of David's regressive behavior within this cultural context. Under the stress of leaving his law firm, where he had performed at a very high-powered level that required a strong drive as well as independent thinking and behavior, David had allowed himself, within the privacy of his home and in his relationship with his wife, to regress. The Jewish home is the haven where hard-driving Jewish men can let down, relax, and allow themselves to be dependent on their wives. It is a transitory state—what psychoanalysts term "regression in the service of the ego"—an opportunity to recharge one's batteries in preparation for the next day's work. Decision-making powers are relegated to the wife in terms of managing the home, child rearing, socializing, and so on. A friend of mine often talked about her grandparents' relationship, in which this dynamic was played out graphically. Her grandfather was a highly successful, multimillionaire businessman who had originally emigrated from Russia as a penniless twelve-year-old. At age twenty-two Dave was married to Rita, the sister of a close friend. "Dave," her grandmother used to say when he made her angry, "you don't know nothing, and you can't do nothing, so keep quiet." And Dave did just that without the slightest sign that he felt put down.

Joan, however, did not have the cultural experience to understand this. All she knew was that David was not allowing her any space during the day and, furthermore, was attempting to squelch her individuality by overpowering her with his religion. Her sudden interest in Episcopal Christianity was an obvious reaction to this. She also had not understood David's bond to his father and the rest of his family. She incorrectly interpreted this behavior as "codependency," rather than culturally pat-terned interdependence. Joan also interpreted his mother's fre-quent visits, which had become insufferable, as signs of David's inability to separate emotionally from his parents. The situation became totally impossible when David's mother tried to control her daughter-in-law. The rage that Joan felt, but was able to control, was intense.

After two individual sessions with Joan, when she had let go of a great deal of her accumulated anger, I felt that we had to in-clude David in the treatment. She balked at this suggestion at first. She was getting relief, she said, by seeing me alone; she felt outnumbered by her husband's family and needed an ally of her own. I empathized with this and yet was able to prevail, so we arranged for a conjoint session the following week.

David is a soft-spoken, relaxed man, carefully dressed, light complected with blue eyes, slightly overweight, who seemed to me the prototypical WASP professional man. He related in a warm, thoughtful manner and took a passive, condescending posture toward his wife, who sat next to him on the couch. They looked good together, I thought. She looked very much the suburban matron, expensively dressed, with only slight traces of an English accent. She is about the same height as her husband, has sharp facial features and long brunette hair falling onto her shoulders.

I focused on David in this initial conjoint session, asking him what he thought the problem between them was. It was amazing to me what little insight into their issues this highly educated man had. He started by complaining that his wife had little empathy for him. In order to justify this feeling, he related a recent incident: He had been home ill with a terrible flu, and his distress was so intense that he considered being hospitalized, but Joan could barely get herself to bring him soup and medicines.

Joan was visibly impatient as her husband related this story. In a casual, nondefensive way, she explained that David's illness was the last straw in a chain of unrelenting demands he had been making on her. She had sensed that nothing serious was wrong with him—and yes, she could not get herself to minister to him one second longer. Furthermore, she felt he was exaggerating his pain, as usual—being regressive and dependent, as usual. She added defiantly that she had absolutely no guilt about her behavior. David looked at me hoping, I thought, that the outrageousness of his wife's stance was apparent to me. I responded by sympathizing that the experience must have been disheartening for him. I then wondered out loud how things between them had gotten so bad. It was clear that each blamed the other. Joan had already had her day in court in our individual sessions, and now David was presenting his rebuttal. This, attributing the source of one's pain to the flaws of one's spouse, was a characteristic maneuver of couples in marital distress. There are other ways, however, of understanding what has gone wrong between them.

Gradually, over the following sessions, I introduced them to an alternative cultural perspective from which to view their conflicts. They both firmly resisted my culturally oriented interpretations, especially David. Having attended the best American schools, he considered himself fully socialized in American values and norms. In fact, even the prestigious law firm he had worked for was predominantly WASP. He didn't like to have his Jewish heritage used to explain his wife's emotional sterility and lack of empathy. He also expressed his belief that I was siding with his wife against him. I was afraid he was going to lose faith in me and terminate treatment, but we weathered these misperceptions and were able to concentrate on both Joan and David, gaining the "broadsight" to redefine the issues that divided them in cultural terms. When Joan realized David's "dependency" was in fact not a character flaw but a culturally learned trait, she relaxed.

It was a joy for me to see the tension between them gradually decrease as their understanding grew. Joan was now able to both tolerate and set limits on David's "dependency" without the defensive rage she had experienced before. She also set limits on his mother's visits, which David could now support. He also decided that his practice had grown sufficiently so that he could rent offices in their suburban town.

The children went to Hebrew school and Joan went to church on Sunday. They agreed to let their children make the final decision about religion when they were older. In the meantime, each would be supportive of the other's religious practices. They saw a common need for spirituality in their lives and resolved to satisfy this within and with respect for their respective traditions.

9

FURTHER CLINICAL CONSIDERATIONS

I have attempted to describe the complex interaction of psychological and cultural events as they unfolded in the therapeutic process. I tried to contrast a purely psychological formulation of the presenting problems with one that is expanded and enhanced by a cultural perspective. It becomes evident how an understanding of the ethnic background of the patients and the couples can make a critical difference in an effective therapeutic endeavor. What is especially important is that the individuals and couples studied were third-generation hyphenated Americans, the grandchildren of the original immigrants.

Let me now share with you some of the highlights in the analysis of these cases in order to describe the complex interaction of psychological and cultural factors that are central to a broader understanding of the presenting disorders. Michael Patterson, an Irish-American man, presented with a severe case of post-traumatic stress disorder. This "target behavior" was addressed behaviorally through the employment of appropriate techniques and resolved in a relatively few number of sessions.

Most therapists would have considered him or her significantly improved and not necessarily in need of further treatment.

Furthermore, the patient's Irishness would not have been considered a relevant variable in assessing his problem. What emerged in subsequent sessions, however, through a psychodynamic—that is, insight-oriented—approach was a broad range of conflicts directly related to his confusion about his ethnic identity. While he considered himself totally "American," he had taken a career direction that was in basic ways Irish. He had formed a band with other Irish-American men and earned an income by performing at weddings and piano bars in the Boston area. He had assumed the role of the Irish troubadour without any awareness of having done so.

Furthermore, the family arrangement that had been structured with his wife had developed into a typically Irish, matriarchal system. She was the primary wage earner, having advanced to a high executive position in a business firm. He took care of the children during the day and worked primarily at night. His middle-class mainstream American value orientations, however, conflicted with his house husband role. He, too, was a university graduate who was only dimly aware of a strong drive to achieve professionally. Therapy made it possible for him to access this conflicting issue in his life. Conjoint sessions with his wife, with much reluctance on her part, finally resulted in a restructuring of their roles in their family. He enrolled in the training program of a large bank and prepared himself for a career in the business world. She agreed to return home at a regular and earlier hour of the day to assume more of the parenting functions. They arranged for a day care center so that he could attend to his new career.

Steven Genovese, an Italian-American man, presented with a case of obsessive-compulsive disorder. He engaged in decontamination and checking rituals that significantly impaired his functioning. Again, these symptoms were addressed first through the prescribed behavioral interventions and through the appropriate medications. Since OCD is an anxiety disorder, it was important to identify the source of his problems. This was done, again, through an insight or broadsight oriented approach and with a culturally relevant perspective.

This patient had strong separation anxiety issues. He had been socialized in a tightly knit extended Italian family where interdependence among its members constituted the major form of support and security. He experienced his first OCD symptoms when he left home to attend college. He experienced pervasive anxiety and was barely able to finish the four-year program. In fact, he had stabilized some after an initial anxiety-ridden freshman year, but his symptoms exacerbated when he was approaching graduation and about to experience still another separation.

This man's treatment was focused on helping him move from interdependence in the Italian pattern to a more independent, that is, individualistic, direction. He gradually became aware of the discrepancy between his Italian upbringing and the demands of the mainstream "American" society with which he was interfacing. In addition to acquiring his new for him insight or "broadsight," as I term it, he was encouraged to take steps in an independent direction. This involved getting an apartment of his own and beginning to date women. He had had only minimal experience dating until this time. He was frightened of his sexuality, and his social contacts were limited to male friends and women he was related to in some way—cousins, for instance.

His job search was a major factor in his "acculturation" process. Although he was a university graduate, he at first applied for employment in jobs that were far below his education and capabilities. He had been so anxious about criticism from bosses who would be judging his performance that he leaned toward positions where he felt he could succeed with minimal effort and risk.

He was finally able in the course of therapy to address his anxiety and to move into a position that was more challenging and by definition more satisfying.

The behavioral methods initially employed to address his OCD symptoms directly were enhanced by the "broadsight" he was able to acquire and the resultant decrease in his separation anxiety. Steven also began dating women and experienced his first sexual encounter. He was, of course, initially frightened to approach a woman and felt exhilarated by having overcome the inhibitory barriers that had not allowed him to express his sexuality. He was finally able to draw on his own internal resources for strength and a sense of security. He no longer needed to be dependent on his family totally in a symbiotic way for support.

Dianne Kaplan's conflicts with her husband were perceived by her as purely personality issues. He was to blame because of his insensitivity to her needs to be close to her family. She needed to realize gradually that her demands reflected a perception of family life that typified that of her own Jewish family. Her husband who had moved toward the internalization of American value orientations insisted on distancing himself, in an individualistic way, from his in-laws.

Dianne's struggle for independence with her own father is a clear example of intergenerational culture conflict. He insisted she date only Jewish men. She rebelled, but in the end married a Jewish man. While her choice of a spouse was not limited to his being Jewish, it reflected her ambivalence. She too wanted a Jewish home, but she also wanted to be independent from any constraints she perceived that her husband imposed on her. While this is clearly a "transference" issue, she projected onto her husband her father's behavior, it also reflects the conflicting needs of being both an independent career person and a wife and mother in a Jewish family.

The successful therapeutic outcome in the case of the Greek-American patient, Bill Anastos, was clearly related to his addressing the culture conflict that characterized his life. His severe anxiety disorder was caused by his effort to move out of the Greek world in which he grew up and to adapt to American core culture in terms of both work and love. His dependency on his mother was not merely a characterological problem. He was conditioned to believe that, as a Greek son, he had the obligation to meet his mother's emotional needs. He also felt protected by her and experienced intense anxiety when he tried to separate from her. This symbiotic bond was reinforced by Greek cultural values—the emphasis on strong family bonds within an authoritarian family structure. In the absence of his father, he was shaped by his mother into the role of "husband" while remaining dependent on her as the dutiful son.

Finally, let us review one of the marital cases that I have described. Disparate cultural expectations had strained seriously the marriage of Tony and Marianne. After a year into their marriage, things began to go painfully bad.

What emerged early in our sessions together was that Tony was furious with his wife because of her emotional unavailability to him. She was working in a large corporation and was highly motivated to succeed in advancing her career. She left early in the morning for work and often returned home after seven in the evening. They had very few meals together. Furthermore, she often left again in the evening to attend courses she needed to enhance her career development. Tony interpreted all of this as her distancing from him. He interpreted her reluctance to visit his parents on some weekends as further evidence of her cold, insensitive nature.

Marianne was bewildered by her husband's stance. She thought they had agreed that each of them would pursue their respective careers—that she did not intend to be a housewife and she did not particularly want children. Tony's conscious desire to separate himself from traditional Italian family patterns was not consistent with his need for the kind of closeness and intimacy he had experienced in his family growing up. His "Italian" value orientations continued to impact on his thinking and feeling. This discrepancy gradually emerged in our conjoint sessions. Each of them was able for the first time to understand where the other was "coming from."

They each made adjustments to meet the expectations of the other. Marianne came home earlier and had dinner regularly with her husband. She also was more empathic about her husband's need to maintain contact with his family—family she was originally made to believe he was trying to get away from. He understood himself better and was able to support his wife's ambition to succeed in her work. He ceased to experience her as uncaring. Their sexual life improved significantly.

The complex interweaving of psychological and cultural factors in the cases reviewed above needs further elaboration. What becomes evident in these cases is that the therapeutic strategy employed by the therapist is not contingent only on the theory of personality that he or she has internalized in the course of training. What is also brought to the therapeutic situation is the underlying value assumptions of the therapist. These mirror the values or value orientations of the society in which he and his patient are members. In this country American mainstream value orientations also guide the therapist in the directions he goes in designing a treatment strategy. He assumes the patient shares these value orientations—that is, he expects the patient to collaborate in their conjoint effort to "work through" his problems (Doing) in order to become more independent (Individualism) sometime in the future (Future). Furthermore, the therapist assumes his patient believes that all problems have solutions (Mastery-over-nature). Also, his relationship to the patient is based on egalitarianism that is consistent with the goal of helping the patient become more independent.

In fact, however, and often outside the awareness of both the therapist and the patient, their relationship is better characterized as Lineal. The therapist remains the doctor who controls in a covert manner the direction the treatment is going irrespective of his theoretical commitment—be it psychoanalytic or behavioral or the many other theoretical systems in between. In cases where the therapist and patient have the same cultural value orientations, they are able to communicate well so that the major focus is on the psychological conflicts of the patient. There is basic agreement on the goals of their therapeutic enterprise—specifically for the patient to become more functional in the areas of love and work at some time in the future. This reflects the fact that they share the Doing, Individualism, and Mastery-over-nature orientations.

When this congruence in cultural value orientations is not present, however, the patient-therapist relationship is compromised. The therapy does not progress in the manner both had hoped for. Both feel their expectations are not met. The patient is confused since he or she does not know how to meet the expectations of the therapist. The therapist labels him or her as "resistant" so that the treatment rapidly reaches an impasse and fails.

Specifically, patients whose ancestry derives from Southern Europe, rural areas of Hispanic-speaking countries, and some Asian countries bring a conflicting pattern of value orientations to the therapeutic situation. It is more likely that in their socialization they have internalized first-order Being, Collateral, Present-time, and Subjugated-to-nature orientations. Consequently, they are unlikely to conceptualize their emotional difficulties as psychological problems that require an expert for them to be helped in solving them. In other words, they do not bring to the treatment situation the concept of psychological causality, which is based on a Doing, Mastery-over-nature and Future orientation. Instead they understand their difficulties as organically based so that they often present with psychosomatic symptoms. They view themselves as victims of an illness over which they have no control (Subjugated-to-nature). They expect the doctor, who is perceived in an authoritarian role (Lineality), to give them medication to "cure" their problem.

Conflicts between individuals are understood as reflecting the Evil nature of one or the other of those involved. Serious mental illness such as schizophrenia is often understood as demonic possession. The priest is called upon to exorcise the devil in order to free the individual from his or her malady.

It becomes obvious that the therapist must be able cognitively and emotionally to separate himself from his own biases—that is, value orientations—in order to be able to address his patient's issues. His capacity to be empathic toward the patient is contingent on his ability to do so.

It is also important for the therapist to be able to assess where his patient is positioned on the acculturation continuum. Is the patient primarily ensconced in his ethnic community where primary relationships are with other members of his subculture? Or is he or she an individual who is primarily motivated to succeeding in the broader "American" community—that is, who is upwardly mobile? These two disparate directions require appropriate intervention approaches. The rapidly acculturating individual needs to be helped to cognitively disentangle the values of the ethnic community in which he or she grew up from those of the core American society in which he or she plans to live and work. The resolution of his "culture conflict" is contingent on an identification of the discrepant value orientations and the specific behaviors they generate. Often compromises need to be struck between the conflicting demands of Individualism and Lineality, for example. Respect for one's elders would need to be integrated with the independence required for making it in American society.

A too rapid abandonment of traditional—that is, ethnic—values in the acculturation process can result in traumatic emotional difficulties such as anxiety and depression. The therapist can guide this individual to avail himself or herself of the emotional resources—support from family and friends—that can buffer the emotional impact of culture change. When such patients are able to accept in themselves those aspects of their ethnic heritage that consolidate their sense of identity, they will be strengthened to cope with the demands of a technologically advanced social system.

With regard to an individual who is firmly imbedded in his ethnic community, the goals of therapy would be quite different. Efforts to move him or her in the direction of adapting to mainstream value orientations would be ineffective. The therapist needs to distinguish such individuals from those who are actively seeking to acculturate. A classification of the discrepancy between ethnic and mainstream American values could lead to confusion. The main focus should instead be to support this individual in resolving the presenting problems such as family or intergenerational conflict within the context of the ethnic community itself.

SOCIAL CLASS VARIATIONS IN VALUE ORIENTATIONS

It is also important to note that value orientation discordance is not limited to members of ethnic groups undergoing the acculturation process. It is identifiable in the interactions between social classes in America as well as in other parts of the world. Working-class individuals often find themselves in conflict with those of the middle class. Their primary Being orientation often is evident in their concept of time. Their Present-time orientation can be exasperating to an employer or an individual they are doing work for. Punctuality is not a primary value; therefore, their not showing up on a scheduled day to perform a service is viewed by the client as irresponsibility. The working-class person feels it is appropriate to change direction in the course of the day if a new opportunity presents itself.

Traditional modes of psychodynamically oriented treatment approaches have been consistently ineffective in treating working-class individuals. Similarly, with ethnic Americans who come from agrarian societies, their focus on Being, Collaterality or Lineality, Present-time, and Subjugated-to-nature results in discordant expectations in the psychotherapeutic situation. The problem is often blamed on the patient who is labeled "resistant."

When treating the working-class patient, the therapist again has to reexamine his traditionally patterned role. Taking a more Lineal—direct—approach in the therapeutic situation could be effective when his patient has been socialized to listen to and respect authority.

The current emphasis in mental health on short-term therapy, promoted by human resources organizations, is consistent with the working-class Present orientation. The current emphasis, also, on psychopharmacology is consistent with the propensity to see emotional distress as an organic problem—as do some ethnic Americans.

REGIONAL VARIATIONS IN VALUE ORIENTATIONS

There are also regional variations in value orientations in this country. While it can be misleading to characterize one section of the country as reflecting a particular pattern of value orientations, most would agree that there are clear differences between the deep rural South and the urban North. The South is more traditional with a greater emphasis on formal characteristics of social position and age—that is, a respect for authority—which reflects a Lineal orientation in the relational area.

A personal anecdote will describe this difference. When I recently mentioned to a colleague of mine that I was planning to visit Charlottesville to give a lecture at the University of Virginia, he responded by commenting that I would experience a different culture there. He said that Jeffersonian democratic values still permeate the town, that a trusting bond connects people, and that when students at the University of Virginia want to cash a personal check, banks do not ask for an ID. To further support this view, he related to me a personal incident. While visiting with his family some years ago, he found himself early one morning walking, alone, on a main street of the town. He looked up to see five young men walking towards him. Their heads were cleanly shaven, and they were all over six feet tall. His first impulse was to turn around and head back to the hotel. For some reason he decided not to and as these men approached, he thought to himself, "Here it comes." Instead what happened was that the young men stepped aside and let him pass. As they did so, they politely wished him, in unison, a good morning.

My friend's perception of the situation—his feelings (panic) and his behavior (the tendency to want to run)—were shaped by his knowledge and experience of similar situations in a northern, urban environment. There his reaction, his thinking, his feeling, and his intended action would have been adaptive. In Charlottesville it was inappropriate.

THE CORPORATE WORLD VARIATIONS IN VALUE ORIENTATIONS

I would like now to shift our focus and to examine some of these same cultural variables in the context of corporations and other institutions.

Mainstream American value orientations can be expected to characterize business organizations as well since to a great degree they are managed by and are constituted by individuals socialized in American culture. To quote Edgar Schein,

> Discussion of American business culture generally centers on how the cultural heritage of the larger society influences the business environment; frequent reference is

made to deeply rooted American individualism, frontier psychology, religious perceptions of good and evil, desire to master the environment, confrontational approach to problems, directness in interpersonal relations, and future orientation.[1]

There are, in fact, wide variations from this norm in the culture values that undergird American corporations—just as there are variations in different regions of the United States and indeed in different professional subgroups and special interest groups of all kinds in this country. Also, professed values are not always the values that are actually operative in corporate social structures. Some corporations are clearly lineally oriented. They are characterized by a dominant-submissive mode of relating. This takes the form of an adversary relationship between management and the on-line workers. Unions advocate for workers when conflict with management occurs. This reality belies the overt Individualism-Collaterality that characterizes American culture as a whole.

Other corporations are indeed organized around mainstream—democratic—values. Workers are given responsibility to regulate their work conditions, and collateral—interdependent—relationships between management and labor are encouraged.

The acculturation process that characterizes American ethnic groups is paralleled in American corporations—through a variety of sources such as downsizing, acquisitions, and mergers. An acquiring company's value system, for example, may differ widely from that of the company being acquired. Confusion, anxiety, and disorganization can occur when the ground rules of conducting business suddenly change. The discordance between the management styles of two merging companies can result in indecision and paralysis. When the ground rules are no longer clear as to which behavior results in advancement and which results in demotion, apathy and demoralization develop among personnel.

Changing work conditions also demands shifts in priorities and strategies within a company that, in turn, are predicated on culture change. Abandoning traditional ways of doing things—such as a major focus on quality—and a de-emphasis on quantity—can result in the loss of a competitive edge.

Effective adaptation to the new business environment facing a company requires, then, a shift in cultural values that parallels the acculturation process in American ethnic groups.

A prime example of a successful acculturation focus on industry is the establishment of automotive plants in the United States by Honda and Nissan. The work culture they promoted was at variance with that of more traditional modes of Lineal—that is, authoritarian—management styles based on adversary labor-management relations and severe work rules. Instead they trained workers for interdependence, or Collaterality—teamwork where supervision is minimal. Each team is autonomous and self-managed; work rules tend to be flexible, and pay is tied to increasing levels of competence.

Just as immigrants and their children are resocialized in the value orientations of the new American society to which they are attempting to adjust, corporations that are sensitive to this issue instigate culture change operations in their organizations. They anticipate the disorganization that can occur, and so they provide workshops and other programs to orient their personnel to the cultural changes that are occurring. Extant systems of development and training are employed to inculcate core values and beliefs.

The complex task of culture changes at the Equitable is described by Kathleen Dechant:

> In shifting from a conservative hierarchically organized insurance company compared to an aggressive provider of diverse financial services, the Equitable decentralized, re-

organized, and undertook a major culture change. New entrepreneurial values were needed in the new marketplace—a willingness to take risks, to innovate, to work in teams so as to optimize available talent. In planning the change, the Equitable identified several "levers of change." Leadership, training, communication, structure, reward, and selection were identified and furthermore specified the task of each. The job of preparing the organization for new values and skills was assigned to the corporate human resources department.[2]

Another example of a marked shift in cultural values is the psychotherapy industry. Traditionally psychotherapists in this country were trained in psychoanalytically oriented therapy. This mode of therapy is based on an elaborate theoretical system in which one's focus is on long term, future-oriented, intrapsychic explorations and the uncovering of suppressed—that is, unconscious—events in the early life of the patient. This process could take a long time and many sessions. With the advent of managed care and health maintenance organization, however, this method became dysfunctional. The emphasis has now shifted to short-term, symptom-oriented interventions. Training programs now emphasize approaches that promise change in a limited number of sessions. Psychopharmacologic medications like Prozac have become standard in the treatment not only of psychotic disorders but of neurotic disorders as well. Traditionally trained psychotherapists are disillusioned by these changes. When they trained, the highest value was placed on excellence in the delivery of service—quality, if you will. The new value is on cost-effective approaches; reinforcement for quality of service is absent.

Psychotherapists who ignore managed care and HMOs find themselves outside the mainstream of referrals, their existence threatened. Some are resourceful and find ways to survive in spite of the changes that are occurring. Others do not.

NOTES

1. E. H. Schein, *Organizational culture and leadership*, 2nd ed. (San Francisco: Jossey-Bass, 1992).
2. K. Dechant, quoted in ibid.

10

CULTURE CHANGE IN AMERICAN SOCIETY

Finally, let us examine briefly culture change as it relates to the "new immigrants" who now constitute a significant proportion of the work force in America. In the last decade, that is 1981–1990, 7.3 million people, predominantly Hispanic and Asian, immigrated to the United States. In the 1990s, 8.5 million immigrants are expected. (At the peak of the European migration at the turn of the century, 8.8 million people emigrated from Europe, 8 million of whom were white.)

This new influx of immigrants is changing the demographics of this country. In the Los Angeles area whites are already outnumbered by ethnics, primarily Latinos and Asians.

These new immigrants with their varying cultural value orientations have impacted on the traditional American core culture. These groups have developed ethnic enclaves in major American cities, as did immigrant groups before them. New York City, for example, now has neighborhoods that are distinctly Hispanic, Korean, Vietnamese, Greek, and so forth. They tend to be characterized by Being, Collateral, and Present-time orientations. Mainstream Americans are drawn to these cultural forms as a kind of relief from the strain of Doing, Individualism, Future-time, and Mastery-over-nature value orientations. While these groups may, in fact, be achievement oriented—engaging in small businesses, buying property, etc.—they paradoxically maintain a strong Collateral orientation. This is evident in their strong family ties; they spend more time together and enjoy the company of extended family, neighbors, and friends.

The reexamining of the Protestant work ethic is becoming more evident among mainstream Americans, especially those working in white-collar positions in large corporations. While it is certainly not a national trend, a significant number of these individuals are choosing to downgrade their work commitments, and the corollary decrease in income, to be able to spend more time with their families.

This emerging shift in value orientation preferences in the nineties parallels the profound culture change that took place in this country in the sixties. This "cultural revolution" resulted in profound changes and constituted a direct challenge to the traditional values that dominated the society at that time.

The challenge was two-pronged. First, the Protestant ethic itself was being questioned for demanding individual achievement at the cost of other human needs, principally in the aesthetic and affective areas—that is, the Being, Collateral, Present-time, and Harmony-with-nature value orientations. The second aspect of this challenge was the unmasking of the covert authoritarian relational values that pattern institutional arrangements in much of American society. Behind the overt Individual > Collateral > American institutions, it has become apparent that a covert Individual > Lineal > Collateral pattern exists. Though Individualism continues to be the first-order preference in this covert pattern, it is backed by a second-order Lineality, while Collaterality is relegated to a third-order position. Supposedly abhorring authoritarianism in any form, Americans, in fact, function in hierarchically structured settings. The school system, for instance, teaches children to be individualistic and independent while the system itself is administered through a hierarchy that includes a superintendent, principals, department heads, and so on. Administrative decisions, to be sure, are arrived at through numerous committees that provide the trappings and feeling of a second-order Collaterality. However, in the last analysis, one's position in the hierarchy determines how much power one can employ in decision making for the system as a whole.

A close look at the social structure of industry, of bureaucratic agencies, and of the executive and legislative branches of the federal government confirms the point. Although the Constitution is based on the principles of open elections, majority rule, and a balance of power between the executive, legislative, and judicial branches of government, the observance of these principles in practice does not conform in all respects to the intentions of its authors. The country's democratic institutions, it seems, are not as democratic as has been believed.

Awareness of the high cost of demanding achievement above everything and of the gap between democratic theory and authoritarian practice has been stimulated by various social movements originating in the 1960s. These movements were mobilized for the purpose of confronting one or the other of these two aspects of American culture. The so-called youth movement of the sixties clearly was guided by both of the above considerations.

The issues that motivated youth to take group action against the "system" varied. Young people protested against the war in Vietnam, discrimination against minority groups, pollution of the environment by large industries, and "authoritarian" administrative structures in a broad range of institutions. These protests ranged from direct confrontation—sometimes violent—

against the power structure in high schools and universities to peaceful demonstrations such as those staged in the nation's capital against the war in Vietnam. Alternative lifestyle arrangements and various communal patterns also constituted in part a protest and a clear rejection of middle-class norms. The drug subculture represented another way of "dropping out" from the system. Timothy Leary urged his audiences to "tune in, turn on, and drop out," and the thousands that followed his direction created a major social problem in our times. The appeal of the encounter group movement with its emphasis on the expression of feelings and learning to be oneself reflected the perception that the established modes of interaction in our society do not provide adequate opportunity to meet these needs.

The themes that undergirded the various manifestations of rebellion against the "system" are not difficult to discern. The dominant one is a growing awareness among young people of the discrepancy between the professed values of their society, which they internalized in their formative years, and the actual functioning of the various institutions that confront them as they reach maturity. Though conflict between the old and the young has cropped up at all times and in all places, its manifestations in the United States in the 1960s had far-reaching effects on the evolution of the culture itself. What was at issue here was not principally the abhorrence of authoritarian values themselves. That was taken for granted. What produced outraged response was the discovery that the national behavior was at variance with what they had been socialized into believing was the reality. The cognitive dissonance that this realization created and the pain that it engendered found its expression in various manifestations of protest against the "establishment." The unbearable dissonance needed to be resolved. Things had to be made "right" again.

The momentum provided by the youth movement spread to other issues as well. The women's liberation movement is a visible example. The drive for equal rights for women, originating late in the nineteenth century, became an effective social movement in the 1960s. Male chauvinism was the immediate target of attack; the social system that relegated women to an inferior status was the main focus of the movement. Women organized effectively to change hiring practices and salary scales. They vociferously challenged the role of mother and housewife assigned to them and fought successfully for the right to be viewed in terms of individual merit and not of gender. The success of their continuing effort is evidenced in the increased frequency with which women now appear on boards of directors of large corporations, in prestigious government positions, and in other spheres of activity previously limited almost entirely to men.

The youth movement of the 1960s was not limited to a challenge of the authoritarian—that is, the third-order Lineal, value orientations that patterned the relational area in American culture. It was directed also to the reexamination of the value orientations that patterned life in the other areas, such as the activity, time, and man-nature modalities. The Protestant work ethic with its emphasis on achievement (Doing > Being > Being-in-becoming), on planning for the future (Future > Present > Past), and on overcoming problems by technological means (Mastery-over > Subjugated-to > Harmony-with) also was brought into question. These middle-class orientations, it was felt, did not produce the happiness and sense of individual fulfillment that they promised. Young people had only to look at the older generation to find confirmation for their emerging doubts. The youth movement provided a stage for experiencing value orientations that were not available to them through conventional lifestyles. These were the Being, Collateral, Present-time, and Harmony-with-nature orientations. The emergence of these value orientations as the preferred patterns for living is described in Kenniston.[1] In the summer of 1967, an organization called Vietnam Summer was organized by young men and women for the purpose of opposing the war in Southeast Asia. Kenniston was asked to study the group from a sociopsychological perspective, and in the course of doing so, he interviewed several members. Revealing insights emerged.

These young radicals were not motivated in their antiestablishment efforts by a clearly formulated political ideology. The New Left was not interested in attacking the capitalistic system as such and was not interested in an alternative, socialistic political philosophy, as some of its critics have suggested. Its adherents talked instead of the alternate ways of experiencing life that their movement provided. It allowed them to recognize and express a broad range of emotions that were previously neglected or shunned in conventional settings. Individualistic needs were subordinated to group purposes, freeing the individuals involved to "be themselves." No longer burdened by any strivings for success in career terms, they could dedicate themselves instead to effecting changes in what they saw to be an unjust system. This made it possible for them to enhance their individuality and discover the unique emotional and intellectual resources they already had instead of shaping their behavior to meet the demands of the marketplace.

These views are expressed in the comments of one person interviewed by Kenniston, who was asked by him whether she had ever thought about abandoning the work of the movement:

No, I've been really very happy. This is one of the things I feel very positive about. . . . One of the things I've learned in the last two years is that you don't need very much to live on. . . . It gives me a completely different perspective on what it is that I decide to go into. I wouldn't mind having a car, but I would have to learn to drive first. I can think of ways to enjoy a nice way of life, but I don't feel obsessed by it. . . .

I sort of feel myself to be open and I feel very happy. It is like I have built a whole new world. It has been a very good transition. I feel I have a solid foundation. . . . I just saw a friend of mine from ten years ago the other day, and it was very difficult to talk to her. . . . You realize that the people you want to be your friends are the people where you don't have to go through the whole process of justifying why you're doing what you're doing. . . . You end up eliminating a lot of your old friends. . . . The kind of people who get involved in the movement are really people who have a strong need for friendship. . . . I don't feel as politically conscious as maybe I should. Maybe I'm approaching things much more pragmatically. How do you build something? How do you get things done?[2]

The value orientations underpinning these expressions of a new philosophy of life are readily seen. They reflect a commitment to a Collateral orientation as the preferred mode of interpersonal relations and the abandonment of the first-order Individualism that characterizes American core culture. This Collaterality is buttressed by acceptance of the Being-in-becoming over the Doing orientation. The spontaneous experience of individuality in the group is preferred over Doing in the sense of working for the achievement of individual goals independently. And the major time focus of the movement is the Present; changes must take place now and not in some distant Future. The Mastery-over-nature orientation, with its emphasis on technological competence to overcome problems, is dropped in favor of a Harmony-with-nature emphasis.

Kenniston also points out another important feature of the attitudes expressed by members of the New Left. They believed that the new radicalism they were advocating was, in fact, consistent with the basic philosophy of America—a philosophy from which the country had deviated. They saw their movement as a return to the real values of the past.

For members of ethnic groups in the United States in the sixties, the situation was indeed a confusing one. The American dream they were striving to achieve was being rejected by those Americans who were already in possession of it. Second- and third-generation members of ethnic groups who were striving to make it into the system were confronted with the spectacle of thousands of their contemporaries rushing to leave it in one way or another. In the process of trying to "make it" in American middle-class terms, many ethnics had separated themselves from their own subcultural groups. Now they became aware that their mainstream American contemporaries were advocating a return to those very Being, Collateral, and Present-time orientations that undergirded the ethnic subcultures they were leaving.

The sense of alienation experienced by America's radical youth and their efforts to find meaning through the formation of various movements, that is, subcultures of their own, provided the impetus for "hyphenated" Americans to reexamine their own particular heritages in a different light. What was previously viewed as an impediment to their striving for upward social mobility was now seen as a resource they could turn back to in order to reaffirm their own distinctiveness and "personhood."

African-Americans took the lead in this direction. In the early days of the civil rights movement in the 1950s, the major goal of Martin Luther King and his followers was the integration of the African-American population with the rest of American society. His crusade was a continuation of the work of the National Association for the Advancement of Colored People (NAACP), which had labored for many years to combat anti-Negro prejudice in the United States and further the opportunities for African-Americans to gain a firm position in American society.

This vision, however, led to disillusionment in the sixties. Integration, it was argued by many African-Americans, was not proceeding fast enough in spite of the Supreme Court decision of 1954. Despite new opportunities for upward social mobility, the dissatisfaction of African-Americans showed signs of increasing rather than decreasing. The riots of the mid-1960s gave testimony to the rage felt by African-Americans at the discrimination they had experienced over the past century. The eruption of violence in Watts and Newark gave full vent to this rage. As the violent protests in the African-American ghettos mounted, the push for full integration into the American social system lost its momentum. Militant African-American leaders argued for a movement toward separatism, the rejection of the white society that had for so long rejected them. Some of the more extreme advocated a return to Africa, while the majority looked to strengthening the African-American community itself and developing its economic and social resources. Social scientists took positions on opposite sides of the integration-segregation controversy that emerged.

The African-American community, then, intensified the two-pronged challenge to American core values discussed above. They opposed both the overt Individual > Collateral > Lineal and the covert Individual > Lineal > Collateral. The African-American example helped to counteract the sense of alienation experienced by many Americans. The isolation and loneliness, the muting of spontaneity and joy that the Doing and Individualistically oriented middle-class society required, was counterbalanced by the Being, Collateral, and Present-time orientation of the African-American subculture. This does not mean that strivings for individual achievement were abandoned. It means, rather, that the consolidation of the African-American subculture provided an "in-group" where spontaneous feeling could be expressed, where one's sense of individual value could be affirmed, and where one could be psychologically strengthened to cope with the demands of the Protestant work ethic more effectively. Individual achievement now was experienced within the context of a first-order Collateral orientation. One's individual achievements now became a reflection of group membership, of African-American identification that enhanced the status of all African-Americans.

White ethnic groups reacted initially with hostility to the African-American movement. Lower-income groups continued to resist the expansion of the African-American community into previously all-white neighborhoods. The inroads made into previously all-white labor unions also created anxieties and predisposed many negatively to the African-American movement. However, a developing corollary to the consolidation of the African-American community gradually became evident. This development was the emergence of white ethnic groups reaffirming themselves as distinctive minorities.

While white ethnic groups have always maintained subcultures of their own in America, they have rarely taken open stands to emphasize those characteristics that distinguish them from mainstream Americans. The trend, rather, had been to de-emphasize differences in accordance with the "melting pot" demands of American core culture in the occupational and social spheres. The reinforcement of one's ethnic identity was reserved by hyphenated Americans, if at all, for associations within their respective subcultures. Many ethnics were associated with institutions of their subculture from birth until death and took their primary social relations from among members of their own ethnic group.

Cultural pluralism, then, as Gordon[3] and others[4] described it was certainly always a reality on the American scene. The reality of it, however, was rarely advocated overtly as the preferred mode of living. Ethnics viewed themselves as Americans of this or that background, and reference by others to their ethnicity was felt, at best, to be an act of bad taste. There is a dearth of research by social scientists on this reluctance to be studied as an ethnic subculture. Undoubtedly, this sensitivity derives from the aversive consequences of being viewed as "foreign"—that is, different and alien.

This picture began to shift in the sixties. The vociferous determination by African-Americans to be valued because of, rather than in spite of, the color of their skin earned the respect of white ethnics in whom a responsive chord had been struck. A trend now became evident. Ethnic groups began to assert themselves in terms of the distinctiveness of their cultural background.

The African-Americans were followed in this trend first by the Mexican-Americans and by the American Indians. The talk was of Brown Power and Red Power. The Chicano movement in the Southwest was organized around the issue of the exploitation of migrant Mexican-American farm workers by their white employers. Under the dynamic leadership of Cesar Chavez, broader issues relating to the economic territorial rights of Mexican-Americans in the Southwest were later raised. A direct challenge was mounted against the past and present exploitative practices of the United States government, which was accused of illegally appropriating lands that rightfully belonged to Mexican-American farmers and either leasing them to white farmers or designating them national forest. The Chicano movement took on a more comprehensive character in the form of the open assertion of pride by Mexican-Americans in their heritage. They served notice that the stereotype of the lazy Mexican basking in the sun under his sombrero would no longer be tolerated. Mexican-American studies programs appeared in universities in the Southwest where young second- and third-generation Mexican-Americans rediscovered their heritage and identified in a new way with the culture of their forefathers.

The American Indian also asserted himself. Loss of territorial rights, humiliation by the Bureau of Indian Affairs, and any number of long-endured injustices became fighting issues. The squalor of the reservation could no longer be tolerated. Indian leaders attacked the stereotype of the Indian savage scalping women and children until he is brought down by the guns of the hearty Western frontiersman. With the American Indian

Movement (AIM), the cause of Indian rights was reaffirmed on the foundation of Indian history and culture. Indian studies programs now were revitalized in schools on reservations. American Indian intellectuals came forth to lend their support to a group effort to improve the educational standards of schools supported by the Bureau of Indian Affairs and to institute courses on American Indian history and culture in colleges and universities.

The directions taken by white ethnics in asserting their cultural identity varied from those taken by African-Americans, Mexicans, and Indian-Americans. Discrimination against Italians, Irish, Greeks, Poles, and Jews was, after all, not institutionalized in the manner that it was for the more culturally distinct groups, at least not in the sixties. Though the larger groups, such as the Italians, the Irish, and the Jews, had long controlled pockets of the political power in the different cities and states in which they lived, this became manifest only during election periods. The rest of the year the existence of clearly defined enclaves of ethnics in their various neighborhoods throughout the cities and states was an invisible reality. After elections a kind of mass denial was reinstituted by both the ethnics and "mainstream" American society that any differences could be discerned in the cultural composition of the "American people."

Denial had a functional purpose. It facilitated the steady progress being made by white ethnics toward securing for themselves a permanent place in the economic and social structure of America. Trade unions were their domain in some parts of the country. Life was good in the 1960s: a blue-collar worker could earn good wages and provide well for his family; he could buy many of the material goods he was exposed to in the marketplace; and he could even think of putting money aside to send his children to college. Furthermore, the road to upward social mobility was more accessible to white ethnics. The first post–World War II generation reached college age in the 1960s, and the numbers of second- and third-generation "hyphenated Americans" who went to college, the first of their families to do so, increased markedly.

What could be the issues, therefore, around which white ethnics would mobilize to assert their particular cultural distinctiveness? The immediate rallying point seems to have been the threat presented by African-American and Puerto Rican blue-collar workers in large cities who were making significant inroads into previously white ethnic neighborhoods and occupations. In these areas, ethnicity had the functional relevance of combating a perceived social and economic threat. Ethnicity represented the bond that held a group together in its effort to maintain the social and economic interests that had been gained, they felt, through hard work and much sacrifice. Of course, ethnicity also resulted in a special kind of bigotry and prejudice. One category of minority group, white ethnics, opposed a second category of minority group, African-Americans, within a social system that was, to a greater or lesser degree, discriminatory toward both.[5,6] It is indeed a paradox that out of this confrontation of African-Americans and working-class whites, the latter found the opportunity to assert their particular ethnic identities and to awaken their sense of group cohesiveness.

And while this happened as a response to the immediate threat of African-American and Puerto Rican encroachments into economic spheres of ethnic white activity, it also represented the surfacing of long-festering resentments against a broader middle-class American social system that tended to devalue the white ethnics' traditional cultural background.[7] The sense of alienation that they felt was now, for different reasons, being articulated dramatically by middle-class college men and women through the youth movement. It was all coming together, it seemed, through the very process of all coming apart in a society marked by group divisions, by violence, and by the erosion of official values.

The acculturation of white ethnics within American core society thus turned out to have been more apparent than real. The surprising fact that emerged in the 1960s was that it was the third-generation ethnics, the grandchildren of the original ethnics, who were the most energetic in turning to their traditional cultural roots and reaffirming their ethnic identities. They were not motivated by any special wish to oppose the African-American and Puerto Rican movements. The primary impetus came instead from the subjective feelings of alienation they had long felt and that they shared with their young counterparts in all the rest of American society who were neither ethnic nor of working-class origins. The Protestant ethic had caught up with them, too.

Both the working-class ethnic on the assembly line and the professional ethnic in the middle or upper class experienced the same dissatisfaction. Their ethnic backgrounds served, in the first instance, as a base against which their current feelings of isolation and anomie were experienced in sharp relief; they had known a different life when they were growing up in their ethnic homes and neighborhoods, and now they remembered it. Feelings of solidarity and spontaneity were sought, a sense of joy in interpersonal relations that were not cultivated for purposes of "connection." In value orientation terms, they were searching for a lifestyle based on a Being orientation within a Collateral relation framework, geared to the Present rather than the Future. This was the third-generation ethnics' alternative to the encounter groups, group family living arrangements, and drugs used by the youth movement in its reaction to traditional core values.

Open manifestation of ethnic feeling took a variety of forms, and varied in intensity, in different white subcultural groups. In New York City, the Italian-American Fraternal Society organized itself to combat the prejudicial stereotyping of Italian gangsters in movie and television films. This program was also positively geared to affirming the contributions made by Italian-Americans to American society. Polish-American cultural and fraternal organizations also took aggressive stands against the mass media for stereotyping their ethnic group. Pulaski Day in the 1960s drew an unprecedented number of second- and third-generation Polish-Americans who in previous years had left the celebration of the memory of the Polish hero in the American Revolutionary War to their fathers and grandfathers.

Greek-Americans organized themselves into a nationwide organization called the Greek Orthodox Youth of America (G.O.Y.A.). It is important to note that the primary impetus for this effort of Greek-Americans did not come from the fraternal and cultural organizations founded earlier by their immigrant fathers and grandfathers. Nor did it come from the Greek Orthodox Church. It came from the second- and third-generation youth themselves who felt the need to unite for the purpose of deepening their sense of Greek consciousness.

Perhaps the most dramatic manifestation of this reaffirmation of ethnic origins was the response of young American Jews to the Israeli-Arab conflict, first in 1967 and then in 1973. The war in 1967 stirred a deep interest in thousands of young American Jews, and the Israeli victory after only six days of fighting was experienced by them as a personal triumph. Many followed up their emotional involvement in this conflict by going to Israel and working, with the clear purpose of making a contribution to Israel. They believed that in the process they were also renewing themselves. It felt right to commit themselves to a cause outside the realm of their individual social and economic advancement. It satisfied the need for the "mutuality" that Erickson had taught them was an essential ingredient of a healthy personality. When the Israeli-Arab conflict was activated again in 1973, the response of American Jews was overwhelming. Young men and women left their schools and jobs and professions and traveled to Israel to participate in whatever way they could.

The movement of members of American subcultural groups toward renewed pride in their ethnic origins then represents part of the broader reaction of the youth of America to the endemic strains present in contemporary society. We have conceptualized these strains in terms of value orientation theory. The strain incumbent in the discrepancy between the overt Individual > Collateral > Lineal and the covert Individual > Lineal > Collateral > value orientation patterns in the relational area, we have argued, is one of the main sources of strain in the American social system. The other is the intrinsic strain in the traditional emphasis on achievement values—that is, Individualism, Doing, Future-time, and Mastery-over-nature orientations, which do not foster group solidarity or Collaterality, individual commitment to group goals, or spontaneous expression of feelings through trusting interpersonal relations and the joy of just Being. However, what are the implications of this theoretical analysis for the future course of adaptation by American ethnic families in the United States?

Sociologists such as Glazer and Moynihan[8] and Gordon[9] have pointed out that the United States has always been a culturally diverse and pluralistic society. The melting-pot notion of ethnic and national groups' eventually amalgamating into a homogeneous culture is not supported by the facts.

Before the African-American movement, Italians, Irish, Poles, Greeks, Jews, and, in particular, the Chinese maintained separate cultural identities in the United States. In the past, however, the maintenance of ethnic subcultures was based partly on the defensive sociopsychological needs of the subculture members. Ethnics affirmed their value and worth as a group in covert or purely symbolic ways in reaction to the discrimination they faced from the White Anglo-Saxon Protestants who preceded them. In the 1960s the situation was quite different. The issue became one of positively affirming ethnic patterns of life to meet a different configuration of socio-psychological needs: those not being met by that white Anglo-Saxon society, which the ethnics had now joined. In addition, many of the second- and third-generation ethnics had achieved middle-class status. Thus, in the 1960s, affirmation of ethnicity was associated with the protection of political, economic, and social interests. Cultural pluralism in the sixties was more than symbols.

Irvine M. Levine, the director of the National Project on Ethnic America of the American Jewish Committee, stated the issue as follows:

> We need to work out a new system of relationships between groups, a new "pluralism" that accepts uniqueness and balances identification with a small group against commitment to society as a whole, while protecting the individual who does not wish to identify as well. America has too often failed to deal honestly with the ethnic group factor, and this has weakened our nation's legitimate claim on its citizens to join in the common good. Fragmentation results not from recognizing difference, but from ignoring it.[10]

The appeal here is for open recognition that ethnic variation is and always has been an integral part of the American social scene. More important, however, the speaker calls for "acceptance" of the uniqueness and value of American subcultural groups on an equal basis with that of the core middle-class culture.

The appeal to a "new cultural pluralism" is a response to the implicit devaluation of differences from the American cultural norms supported by the covert Individual > Lineal > Collateral value orientation profile with its implied "superior-inferior" patterning of group relations within the various subgroups of the society. Ethnic groups were once clearly on a lower rung of a lineal hierarchy in the United States, their position being determined by how closely, through skin color, country of origin, and religion, they approximated the Anglo-Saxon Protestant white norm. The insistence on shifting to the overt, official Individual > Collateral > Lineal pattern evident in the culture protest movements of the 1960s signals the "new pluralism" advocated by Levine. The egalitarian nature of the Collateral orientation dictates that all groups within the system are entitled to equal status and therefore are entitled to assert their individual and collective uniqueness within the broader social system.

This shifting orientation is clearly a first step toward eliciting the commitment of members of divergent subcultural groups, ethnic and otherwise, to a sense of national purpose. The current fragmentation of American society into competing interest groups of divergent cultural and ideological character is certainly not a viable arrangement for either the subgroups themselves or for the country as a whole. The refusal of thousands of American youth to participate in the "immoral" Vietnam War shocked Americans into the realization of how divided they had become on the issue of national purpose and direction.

It is the second aspect of the culture change process in the United States, however, that poses difficult problems for members of ethnic groups in their efforts to adapt to American core society. How can one internalize the value orientations characterizing the agrarian societies that his forebears came from while at the same time trying to find a place in the social and occupational structure of a technologically advanced urban society?[11] Furthermore, what direction will technological society take now that the Protestant ethic has been challenged? Culture change in the United States has clearly not proceeded to the point where Individualism, Doing, Future, and Mastery-overnature orientations have disappeared from the important institutions. How are the alternative value orientations characterizing ethnic subcultures—that is, Being, Collaterality, Present, Harmony-with-nature—to become viable in America? In other words, what can the new pluralism live on, and what are the psychological implications?

In addressing this fundamental question, let us reexamine an aspect of Kluckhohn's value orientation theory that bears on this issue.[12] Though every society has a dominant configuration of values that differentiates it from other societies, it is also true that within a particular society there can be a wide divergence among the different subgroups. Kluckhohn theorizes that variation in cultural value orientations is a necessary condition for the effective functioning of the society itself. Variation would be expected, for example, among different occupational groups within a society. In the United States, entertainers are more Being-oriented than businessmen while artists are more oriented to the Being-in-becoming pattern. Both artists and entertainers, however, tend to be more Doing-oriented than artists living in a more Being-oriented culture such as Greece. There are, furthermore, obvious regional differences within a country of origin so that northern Italians, emigrants from an industrialized area, are likely to be more Individualistic, Doing, Future, and Mastery-over-nature oriented than southern Italians, born in farming areas where Collaterality, Being, Present-time, and Subjugated-to-nature orientations are primary.

The concept of variation in value orientations is not limited to occupational and regional differences within a society. It applies as well to the different stages of development that an individual traverses in the course of his life. It is almost too obvious to state that children everywhere are more Being than Doing oriented and more focused on the Present than the Future, even though these distinctions become blurred very early in middle-class American society through the inculcation of achievement values in school and on the playground. Also, in the United States, middle age blunts the goals of Future and Doing orientations for individuals whose future has decreased in scope and who have attained as much success as they can realistically hope for. The time parameter, then, is important in considering the stresses imposed by value orientations on an individual in the course of his lifetime.

Finally, value orientations vary within individuals during the course of a single day, a week, or a year. Conditions that emphasize one or another are related to the activities in which individuals engage. During working hours, those orientations that fuel competitive, striving, and achieving behavior are in the ascendancy. In recreational situations, usually in the evening and in the company of family members, Being, Collaterality, Harmony-with-nature, and Present-time orientations are more salient. These leisure-time values in the United States, however, are clearly reflective of dominant core values: competitive sports and achievement pursuits are emphasized more than in other societies. Nevertheless, the most dedicated American businessman has periods when he relaxes his Doing orientation and is reinforced by Being.

Such variations in value orientations are manifest in the social role patterns through which individuals function. In functioning as a father, for example, an American middle-class male will show more feeling and give more emotionally than he will in functioning as a wage earner in competition with his peers. In his role as husband, he can be expected to be more Collateral, that is, egalitarian, with his wife than he will be in his relation with subordinates at work. In his relation with parents, he may adopt a more respectful role as son, reflecting the operation of a Lineal orientation. There is fluctuation, in other words, in the salience of one or the other value orientation for the social role in which an individual functions at a particular time.

The implications of these theoretical considerations point to how the new pluralism might affect the culture of the United States. Members of ethnic groups already do behave differently in relations within their respective in-groups. Depending, of course, on the particular ethnic group in question, they can be more spontaneous, freer in emotional expressions, can commit themselves to the attainment of group goals—in short, relate to each other in ways that are sharply at variance with those that characterize their relations with the "outside" American core community. In the past, however, shifting back and forth between in-group and out-group, between ethnic subculture and American core society took a heavy psychological toll on ethnic Americans. In the seven case studies presented in this volume, we tried to illustrate some of the psychological effects that have accompanied the strain of coping with divergent or conflicting value systems and role expectations within a single society. Neurotic compromise responses emerged from the continuing conflict they had to endure.

Now culture change in the United States has made it possible for ethnic Americans to move in and out of their subcultures without the aversive consequences of previous years—and this, it seems to us, can constitute the essence of the new pluralism in the United States. It is now realistic for ethnic Americans to openly accept the variation in value orientations that characterizes their subcultures and to view these variations as positive, as important—indeed, as psychologically healthy. It can even be argued that shifting back and forth between in-group and out-group in this new context constitutes an integrative, ego-strengthening process. It does so because the in-group can now provide a structure in which those psychological needs not met by the achievement-oriented American culture can be satisfied. The strains incumbent in functioning within a psychologically demanding social system can be relaxed within subsystems whose values allow for more Being, Collateral, Harmony-with-nature, and Present-time oriented thoughts, feelings, and behavior.

The new pluralism conceptualized in this fashion constitutes, then, a new kind of buffer against the stress of acculturation faced principally by second- and third-generation ethnic Americans. Acceptance of their subcultures in a conflict-free manner can liberate their energies for identification with broader national purposes and directions. It can also serve another important function, and that is the facilitation of culture change in the United States: the relaxation of those values that undergird the Protestant ethic to the exclusion of humanistic considerations.

The new pluralism can serve a two-way process of cultural modification between ethnic subcultures on the one hand and the American core society on the other. When American ethnics operate within their respective subcultural communities, they do not experience them in pure form. Italian or Greek culture in Boston is clearly not identical to that of contemporary Italy or Greece. In Boston these ethnic communities have been modified to a degree in their essential character by virtue of their existence within an "American" environment. An Italian from Italy moving into the North End of Boston (an Italian neighborhood) would still need to go through a period of adaptation before he would feel comfortable among his Italian-American neighbors. First-generation Greek-Americans who return to Greece in their old age to retire find that they, too, need a period of acculturation to their original homeland. The ethnic experience in the United States, then, is an ethnic-American experience in which the original subcultural values have undergone some degree of shift toward the American core patterns.

The Italian-American in the North End of Boston is more Being and Collaterally oriented than his counterparts in the WASP suburbs but less so than his relatives in rural Italy. Members of Italian-American peer groups in the West End of Boston, described by Gans,[13] may spend long evenings socializing with each other in the manner of their counterparts in Italy, but they still have to get up early the next morning to go to work.

National, political, and economic conditions also affect and condition the status of their ability to earn money and maintain themselves in this society. These factors permeate their existence and interfere with the essential Being and Collateral orientations that they internalized in their Italian-American homes.

By the same token the challenge to core American values by the youth movement has sensitized "mainstream" Americans to the "ethnic experience" as a potential source of personal fulfillment. Ethnic themes have emerged in the theatre, in motion pictures, and in television productions where subcultural variations in behavior are treated in a positive light. The partial transformation of Individual > Lineal > Collateral to Individual > Collateral > Lineal, which has made ethnicity more acceptable in the United States, may also contribute finally to the relaxation of that intolerance in American middle-class core value orientations that has been a source of individual and intergroup strain.

The current wave of immigrants coming to the United States, then, is confronting a society that is markedly changed from that confronting their predecessors. In some basic ways their acculturation process should be less conflictual. The "new pluralism" allows them to maintain their cultural traditions while freeing them also to adjust to mainstream American society. This course has been facilitated by those who came before them. The new immigrants develop ethnic structures, as did their predecessors, from which they move out to engage the wider American society—economically, socially, and politically. These structures include strong family ties, identification with their ethnic neighborhoods, and religious organizations.

NOTES

1. K. Kenniston, *The young radicals* (New York: Harcourt Brace Jovanovich, 1968).

2. Ibid., p. 25.

3. M. M. Gordon, *Assimilation in American life* (New York: Oxford University Press, 1964).

4. N. Glazer & D. P. Moynihan, *Beyond the melting pot* (Cambridge: Massachusetts Institute of Technology Press, 1963).

5. I. M. Levine & J. Herman, The life of White ethnics, *Dissent* *19* (1) (1972, Winter).

6. I. M. Levine & J. Herman, Search for Identity in blue-collar America, *Civil Rights Digest* (1972, Winter).

7. M. Novak, *The rise of the unmeltable ethnics* (New York: Macmillan, 1971).

8. Glazer & Moynihan, *Beyond the melting pot.*

9. Gordon, *Assimilation in American life.*

10. American Jewish Committee, Pluralism Beyond the Frontier, *Report of the San Francisco Consultation on Ethnicity,* San Francisco (1971), p. 16.

11. H. G. Gutman, Work, culture and society in industrializing America, 1815–1919, *American Historical Review* 78 (June 1973).

12. F. R. Kluckhohn & F. L. Strodtbeck, *Variations in value orientations* (New York: Harper and Row, 1961).

13. H. J. Gans, *The urban villagers* (New York: Free Press, 1962).

BIBLIOGRAPHY

American Jewish Committee. (1971). Pluralism beyond the frontier. *Report of the San Francisco Consultation on Ethnicity*, San Francisco.

Barzini, L. (1964). *The Italians*. New York: Atheneum.

Beck, A. (1976). *Cognitive therapy and emotional disorders*. New York: International Universities Press.

Benson, H. (1975). *The relaxation response*. New York: Avon Books.

Bochner, S. (1982). *Culture in contact*. New York: Pergamon Press.

Brislin, R., & Pedersen, P. B. (1976). *Cross-cultural orientation program*. New York: Gardner Press.

Comas-Diaz, L., & Griffith, E. (1988). *Clinical guidelines in cross-cultural mental health*. New York: Wiley.

Corrigan, E. M. (1970). *The Irish*. New York: Simon & Schuster.

Dechant, K. (1992). *Organizational culture and leadership* (2nd Ed.). San Francisco: Jossey-Bass.

De Vore, W., & Schlesinger, E. (1981). *Ethnic sensitive social work practice*. St. Louis: C. V. Mosby.

Diner, H. R. (1992). *A time for gathering: The second migration, 1820–1880*. Baltimore, MD: Johns Hopkins University Press.

Faber, E. (1992). *A time for planting: The first migration, 1645–1820.* Baltimore, MD: Johns Hopkins University Press.

Gans, H. J. (1962). *The urban villagers.* New York: Free Press.

Gaw, A. (Ed.). (1982). *Cross-cultural psychiatry.* Littleton, MA: Wright-PS G.

Giordano, J. (1986). *The Italian American catalog.* New York: Doubleday.

Giordano, J., & Levine, M. (1975). *Mental health and middle America: A group identity approach* (Working Paper Series No. 14). New York: Institute on Pluralism and Group Identity.

Glazer, N., & Moynihan, D. P. (1962). *Beyond the melting pot.* Cambridge: Massachusetts Institute of Technology Press.

Goldstein, S. (1993). *Profile of American Jewry: Insights from the 1990 National Jewish Population Survey.* New York: Center for Jewish Studies, City University of New York.

Gordon, M. (1981, March). Models of pluralism: The new American dilemma. *Annals of the American Academy of Political and Social Science,* 178–188.

Gordon, M. M. (1964). *Assimilation in American life.* New York: Oxford University Press.

Gutman, H. G. (1973, June). Work, culture and society in industrializing America, 1815–1919. *American Historical Review,* 78.

Herz, F., & Rosen, E. (1982). Jewish families. In M. McGoldrick, J. K. Pearce, & J. Giordano (Eds.), *Ethnicity and family therapy* (1st ed.). (pp. 365–392). New York: Guildford Press.

Horney, K. (1937). *The neurotic personality of our time.* New York: W. W. Norton.

Kenniston, K. (1968). *The young radicals.* New York: Harcourt Brace Jovanovich.

Kluckhohn, F. R., & Strodtbeck, F. L. (1961). *Variations in value orientations.* New York: Harper and Row.

Lefley, H., & Pedersen, P. B. (Eds.). (1986). *Cross-cultural training for mental health professionals.* Springfield, IL: Charles C. Thomas.

Levine, I. M., & Herman, J. (1972, Winter). The life of White ethnics. *Dissent.*

———. (1972, Winter). Search for identity in blue-collar America. *Civil Rights Digest.*

Marsella, A. J. (1978). The modernization of traditional cultures: Consequences for the individual. In D. Hoopes, P. B. Pedersen, & G. Renwick (Eds.), *Overview of intercultural education, training and research* (Vol. III). La Grange Park, IL: Intercultural Network.

Marsella, A. J., & Pedersen, P. B. (1981). *Cross-cultural counseling and psychotherapy*. New York: Pergamon Press.

Masters, W. H., & Johnson, V. E. (1970). *Human sexual inadequacy*. Boston, MA: Little, Brown & Co.

McGoldrick, M., Giordano, J., & Pearce, J. (1996). *Ethnicity and family therapy* (2nd ed.). New York: The Guildford Press.

Miller, K., & Wagner, P. (1995). *Out of Ireland: The story of the Irish immigration to America*. Washington, DC: Elliot & Clark.

Moskos, C. C. (1989). *Greek Americans: Struggle and success* (2nd ed.). Englewood Cliffs, NJ: Prentice Hall.

The new face of America—How immigrants are shaping the world's first multicultural society. (1993, Fall). *Time* (Special Issue).

Novak, M. (1971). *The rise of the unmeltable ethnics*. New York: Macmillan.

Papajohn, J. (1982). A case history of a person with obsessive ruminations. *Intensive behavior therapy* (pp. 67–85). Elmsford, NY: Pergamon Press.

———. (1982). *Intensive behavior therapy. The behavioral treatment of complex emotional disorders*. Elmsford, NY: Pergamon Press.

Papajohn, J., & Spiegel, J. P. (1971). The relationship of cultural value orientation change and Rorschach Indices of Psychological Development. *Journal of Cross Cultural Psychology* 2(3), 257–272.

Papajohn, J., & Spiegel, J. P. (1975). *Transactions in families: A modern approach for resolving cultural and generational conflicts*. San Francisco: Jossey-Bass.

Pavlov, I. P. (1941). *Conditioned reflexes and psychiatry* (W. H. Gantt, Trans.). New York: International Publishers.

Pergola, S. D. (1980). Pattern of American Jewish identity. *Demography, 17*, 261–273.

Pinderhughes, E. (1989). *Understanding race, ethnicity and power*. New York: Free Press.

Schein, E. H. (1992). *Organizational culture and leadership* (2nd Ed.). San Francisco: Jossey-Bass.

Scourby, A. (1984). *The Greek Americans.* Boston: Twayne.

Skinner, B. F. (1953). *Science and human behavior.* New York: Macmillan.

Spiegel, J. P., & Kluckhohn, F. R. (1954). *Integration and conflict in family behavior report 27.* Topeka, KS: Group for the Advancement of Psychiatry.

Stamphl, T., & Levis, D. (1967). Essentials of implosive therapy: A learning theory based on psychodynamic behavioral therapy. *Journal of Abnormal Psychology, 72,* 496–503.

Sue, D. (1978, April). World views and counseling. *Personnel and Guidance Journal,* 458–462.

Triandis, H., Malpass, R., & Davidson, A. (1973). Psychology and culture. *Annual Review of Psychology, 24,* 355–378.

Wolpe, J. (1958). *Psychotherapy by reciprocal inhibition.* Stanford: Stanford University Press.

INDEX

About the Author

JOHN C. PAPAJOHN is a senior attending psychologist at McLean Hospital in Belmont, Massachusetts, and a lecturer in Psychology in the Department of Psychiatry at Harvard Medical School. He is also the Honorary Consul of the Republic of Cyprus in Boston, Massachusetts.

ISBN 0-313-30930-2

9 780313 309304

90000>

EAN

HARDCOVER BAR CODE